CONTENTS

INTRODUCTION – THE NEW REGIME

In April 1999 new Rules were introduced to modernise and simplify court procedures and to focus the attention of the legal system onto achieving fairness and justice for litigants. These changes were collectively known as the "Woolf Reforms" after the Lord Chief Justice Lord Woolf.

The Overriding Objective

The courts are now guided by the Overriding Objective, which states

> "The Rules are a procedural code with the overriding objective of enabling the court to deal with cases justly"

"Dealing with a case justly includes as far as practicable

- ❑ Ensuring that the parties are on an equal footing

- ❑ Saving expense

- ❑ Dealing with a case in ways which are proportionate

  - ○ To the amount of money involved

  - ○ To the importance of the case

  - ○ To the complexity of the issues

  - ○ To the financial position of each party

- ❑ Ensuring that it is dealt with expediently and fairly

- ❑ Allotting to it an appropriate share of the court resources while taking into account the need to allo resources to other cases"

A

STRAIGHTFORWARD

GUIDE TO SMALL CLAIMS

IN THE COUNTY COURT

THE SMALL CLAIMS TRACK

PETER WHIMSTER

Straightforward Publishing

Straightforward Publishing

38 Cromwell Road

London E17 9JN

British Library Cataloguing in Publication Data. A Catalogue record for this book is available from the British Library.

ISBN 1899924 19 1

Printed by Redwood Books

Cover design by Straightforward Graphics

Whilst every effort has been taken to ensure that the information in this book is accurate at the time of going to print, the author and publisher cannot accept liability for any errors or omissions contained within or for any changes to the law as it affects small claims in the county court.

Civil Procedure Rules, Practice Directions & Pre-Action Protocols

The procedure in this guide is a summary of the Civil Procedure Rules. The Rules are divided into 53 sections or "Parts". The Rules are supplemented by Practice Directions issued by the Lord Chancellor's Department. The Practice Direction ("PD") relevant to each Part has the same Part number e.g. Part 7 is supplemented by PD7. The overall procedure is further supplemented by Pre-Action Protocols issued by the Lord Chancellor's Department to guide claimants on the procedure to follow before issuing a claim. The only such protocol relevant to a small claim is the Personal Injury Protocol that is also available from the Lord Chancellor's homepage.

The small track rules are in Part 27 printed in Appendix 1. The practice direction relating to this Part is printed at Appendix 2.

The other relevant Parts are as follows

Part 1	Overriding Objective
Part 7	How to start Proceedings – The Claim form
Part 9	Responding to Particulars of Claim – General
Part 10	Acknowledgement of Service
Part 12	Default Judgment
Part 13	Setting Aside or Varying a Default Judgment
Part 14	Admissions
Part 15	Defense & Reply
Part 16	Statement of Case

| Part 20 | Counterclaims |
| Part 27 | Small Claims Track |

Lord Chancellor's Homepage

The above Parts and the associated Practice Directions are available for downloaded in HTML and Word 6 format ZIP files from www.open.gov.uk/lcd. Paper copies (ISBN 011 3801173) and CD-ROM versions (ISBN 011 7819727) of the Rules may be ordered through from HMSO stationary office, telephone 0870-600 5522. All such Practice Directions, Protocols and Forms are Crown Copyright and they are reproduced with the kind permission of the Controller of HMSO.

Forms

Unlike the second edition, this guide does not reproduce the county court forms because these are available from the Lord Chancellor's homepage. Although care has been taken to reproduce the correct forms, the forms printed are reproduced to illustrate and explain the text. The same forms are available free of charge from any county court office.

Gender

For convenience, the masculine gender has been used throughout this book and is in no way intended to indicate bias or sexism.

Important Note: This guide applies to England & Wales. The law and procedure in Scotland & Northern Ireland is different and this guide should not be used in those countries.

How to Contact the Publisher

We very much hope that this guide will prove to be valuable to those who wish to pursue or defend a small claim, in the county courts. If you have any comments concerning the contents and information in this book please do not hesitate to contact Straightforward Publishing at: 38 Cromwell Road, Walthamstow, London E17 9JN.

1

INTRODUCTION TO THE SMALL CLAIMS TRACK

Under the new regime, a "Small Claims Track" has replaced county court arbitrations, and the court forms have been redesigned. Other types of claims have been assigned to the "Fast Claims Track" and "Multi-Track" as matters of greater complexity, or where the claim is for more than £5,000.

The aim of this guide is to explain the procedure by which you can bring or defend a small claim and how to enforce a judgment. This guide is a guide to procedure not a précis on "the law" or "your rights". The small claims track is designed for lawyer-free dispute resolution. The person who wins the case cannot normally recover their solicitors' fees from their opponent other than the fixed costs on the issue of the Claim Form, witness and other expenses. Costs are explained in Chapter 15.

Small claims are heard the county courts by the district judge. The person who is bringing the claim is called the "claimant" and the person he is making the claim against is known as the "defendant". When a hearing has taken place the district judge will reach a decision known as a "judgment". This is a court order, which usually requires certain action such as to pay compensation or "damages" to the claimant or the claim will be dismissed if the defendant is successful.

2

TYPES OF 'SMALL CLAIM'

This chapter reviews the types of claim that could fall under the small claims track. Small claims often result from a breach of contract such as non-payment of an invoice, or breach of express or implied terms, or from circumstances where there is no contract like personal injury (known as "tort"), or for non-payment of a cheque.

The Supplier's Contractual Right to Payment – Express term

Where goods are delivered or services rendered, the supplier or service provider is entitled to the agreed price or agreed payment for the service rendered. If no price has been agreed, the supplier or service provider is entitled to a reasonable sum for the goods supplied or service rendered.

Breach of Contract: Purchaser's Rights

When goods are supplied which do not comply with the contract, or in breach of terms implied by the Sale of Goods Act (see below), the purchaser is entitled to either:-

- Compensation known as "damages", or

- If the breach is serious, to reject the goods and claim damages for financial loss, for example, a refund of the purchase price, or the cost above the agreed purchase price for goods within the terms of the contract, and any additional loss suffered. The compensation claimed would be the purchase price and any other additional loss suffered. In this situation, the contract is discharged, which means that the purchaser is released of his obligation of payment, or

- To reject the goods and affirm the contract, which means that the contract is not discharged and the purchaser requires the supplier to perform the contract and holds the supplier to his contractual obligations. If the contract is not performed, the aggrieved party may sue for breach of contract.

- Section 75 of the Consumer Credit Act 1974 allows the same "purchasers' rights" to be enforced against a credit card company when the goods are purchased by credit card when the balance can be carried forward from month to month. The same rule does not apply to debit cards.

Sale Of Goods Act, 1979 – Implied Terms

The Sale of Goods Act implies certain terms into contracts for the sale of goods. This means that the seller must supply goods, which satisfy certain statutory terms of contract imposed by Parliament. The principal implied terms are:

- The vendor must own the goods or have the right to sell them

If the goods are sold by description they must correspond with that description. This applies to goods which are described in some way by a label or a notice

identifying the kind of goods they are, or to specific goods which the buyer has not seen at the time of the contract and which are bought on the basis of a description.

- Where a seller sells goods in the course of a business the goods must be of satisfactory quality. This is defined as meaning that they must meet the standard that a reasonable person would regard as satisfactory, taking account of any description of the goods, the price (if relevant) and all the other relevant circumstances. The Act lists the following as aspects of the quality of goods; the fitness for the purpose for which goods of the kind in questions are commonly supplied, the appearance and finish, freedom from minor defects, safety and durability. These provisions do not apply to goods of unsatisfactory quality if the fault has been specifically drawn to the buyer's attention before the contract is made

- If the goods are sold by sample the bulk must correspond to the sample in quality and be free from any defect that would not be apparent on reasonable examination of the sample.

If these conditions are not satisfied, the purchaser has the rights specified above, to damages, to rejection and damages, or to affirm the contract and claim damages for loss suffered.

Supply of Goods and Services Act, 1982 – Implied Terms

This Act relates to the supply of services, which includes a vast range of activities, from having your house altered or redecorated, to having your hair dyed, to having your coat dry cleaned. It includes the supply of goods because often when services are supplied with materials, the materials must be of a suitable quality. The supplier of services is entitled to payment of his invoice and if a price has not been agreed he is entitled to a reasonable charge. Even if the work is not of a reasonable standard the supplier may be entitled to a reasonable payment. Where someone acting in the course of a business supplies a service, the purchaser is entitled to receive a service performed with reasonable care and skill and carried out within a reasonable time. If goods are supplied they must be of satisfactory quality and correspond to any description or sample by which they have been sold. If the work or goods are not of a reasonable standard the purchaser must prove that this is the case and may claim the remedies mentioned above. For example a purchaser may be entitled to damages if the work is so sub-standard that financial loss is suffered such as for plumbing or re-wiring which needs to be completely re-done or a coat, which needs to be replaced after cleaning.

The Supply of Goods and Services Act also applies to contracts for the hire of goods although not to hire purchase agreements. Like contracts for sale, contracts for hire have terms implied into them that the supplier of the goods (the bailor) has the right to hire them out, that they correspond to any description or sample by reference to which the contract has been made and that where the goods are supplied in the course of business they will be of satisfactory quality. In addition, there is an implied term that the person who hires the goods (the bailee) will enjoy quiet possession of the goods for the agreed period unless they are taken by the owner or another person with a right or charge over them which the bailee was told or knew about before the contract was made.

Quantum Meruit – when no price is agreed

This is a legal rule that is derived from previous cases rather than the supply of goods and services statute. It translates as "as much as he deserves" and means that if a price is not agreed before the work is completed, or if one party is prevented by the other, in breach of the contract, from completing the work he had contracted to perform then he may claim payment for the done on a quantum meruit basis. A claim can also be made where the other party has voluntarily accepted partial performance.

The Cheque Rule

If a cheque issued to pay for goods or services is subsequently dishonoured, the recipient can base his claim on the cheque and does not have to prove the contract that led to its payment. This is because the cheques, bills of exchange and promissory notes are regarded as independent contracts, separate from the contract for sale. Consequently there are only a few grounds on which a defendant can defend such a claim such of fraud, duress, total failure of consideration and possibly misrepresentation.

Unfair Contract Terms Act, 1977

Contracts often include exclusion clauses, where one side attempts to limit its liability or the rights of the other party in the event of a breach of contract. The Unfair Contract Terms Act makes any clause excluding or limiting liability for death or personal injury void.

Any exclusion clause that restricts or limits the terms implied by the Sale of Goods Act, where one party is dealing as a consumer, is void. This means that the exclusion has no effect.

Any exclusion clause where one party is dealing on standard terms or one party is a business, will only be effective in so far as the person relying on it can prove that it is "reasonable" as defined by the Act which means that the term "shall have been a fair and reasonable one to be included having regard to the circumstances which were, or ought reasonably to have been known to or in the contemplation of the parties when the contract was made". It is for the person alleging that a term or notice is reasonable to show that it is.

Personal Injuries – Tort

Personal injury claims are treated differently to other claims in that they are not automatically referred to small claims track if the damages claimed for "pain & suffering & loss of amenity" exceed £1,000. This is because personal injury cases often raise difficult issues and the parties are more likely to need legal advice and representation the cost of which is not recoverable in small claims. Taking this £1,000 limit into account, £4,000 is the limit on other loss such as loss of earnings. You should consult the court staff about this point before beginning your case and in the case of a permanent or serious injury, you should take the advice of a Solicitor.

Personal injuries can have been caused deliberately but in most cases the claimant seeks to prove that the defendant was negligent. Four points must be proved to establish negligence:

- The defendant owed a duty of care. With regard to personal injuries, everyone should take reasonable care to avoid doing things or failing to do things, which they can reasonably foresee, would be likely to injure people who they ought reasonably to have foreseen as being so affected by their acts or omissions.

- The defendant acted in breach of his duty

- The breach caused the claimant's injury, and

- The injury was reasonably foreseeable, and not a "freak" accident"

- If the claimant was also negligent the court may find that he was guilty of contributory negligence and reduce the damages awarded to reflect the extent to which the claimant was responsible for causing his own injuries.

Breach of Statutory Duty – Tort

There are several areas in which statute imposes a duty on a public body such as a local authority or a private body such as an employer. For example, the case of injury at work, the claimant could claim compensation on the grounds that the defendant acted in breach of the statutory duties imposed by the Health & Safety at Work legislation. These areas are complicated and research should be undertaken before taking legal action. However, in principle, a simple case could be suited to the small claims procedure.

Consumer Protection Act, 1987 – Unsafe Goods

This Act allows action against a "producer" of goods, which are unsafe, and cause personal injury or loss of or damage to property provided the value of the claim is over £275, excluding interest. The term producer includes the manufacturer, anyone who holds himself out as the producer by putting his name or trade mark on the product and an importer of the product into a Member State of the European Community from a place outside the EC in order to supply it to another in the course of his business. The Act does not apply to damage to the defective product itself or damage to any product supplied with a defective component comprised in it. Furthermore, there is no liability unless the product is a type of property ordinarily intended for private use, occupation or consumption and was intended by the claimant mainly for such purposes. A person who suffers damage to his business property must therefore sue on a contract or in negligence.

15

The Occupier's Liability Acts, 1957 & 1984 – Unsafe Premises

The 1957 Act governs the liability of an occupier in respect of personal injury or damage to property suffered by those who come lawfully onto his premises as visitors. An occupier is under a duty to take such care as in all circumstances of the case is reasonable, to see that the visitor will be reasonably safe in using the premises for the purpose for which he is invited or is permitted to be there. An occupier can discharge his duty by warning his visitor of the particular danger provided that the warning is sufficient to enable the visitor to be reasonably safe.

The 1984 Act concerns the liability of an occupier with regard to people other than his visitors in respect of injuries suffered on the premises, due to the state of the premises, or things done or omitted to be done, on them. This includes trespassers and people exercising private rights of way but not those using public rights of way. The occupier owes such people a duty if he is aware of a danger or has reasonable grounds to believe one exists, if he knows or has reasonable grounds to believe that the non-visitor is in the vicinity of the danger concerned or that he may come into the vicinity and the risk is one against which in all the circumstances of the case he may reasonably be expected to offer the non-visitor some protection. An occupier may be able to discharge his duty by taking reasonable steps to warn people of the danger but whether the warning is adequate will depend on the circumstances.

Housing Matters and Nuisance

The Rules mention specific claims such as a landlords claim for disrepair and/or a tenant's claim for return of the deposit. The limit for such a claim to qualify for the small claims track is £1,000 and not £5,000. A claim for non-payment of rent is an obvious example of a claim arising from housing. In this area rather than just seeking damages under the small claims track, claims may be made for an injunction or an order for specific performance i.e. where a court orders a person to do something or to refrain from doing something. Non-monetary claims are not small claims and fall outside the scope of this guide. Up to £260 may be awarded for legal advice obtained in order to bring or defend an injunction or specific performance or similar relief but this does not cover the cost of being represented at the hearing. In such cases, you should instruct a Solicitor.

Limitation Periods

The law imposes time limits, known as limitation periods within which you must commence your case. Time begins to run from the date of the breach of contract or the date of the actionable tort. Tort includes claims for negligence, which are not based on breach of contract, nuisance and occupiers liability. In personal injury cases it runs from the date when the injury was sustained or, if it is later from the date when the claimant first knew of their injuries. The court has the discretion to extend the time available in personal injury cases in certain circumstances.

The time limits are:

Contract   6 years

Defective products (Consumer Protection Act 1987)   3 years

Personal injury   3 years

If you are the defendant and the claimant's claim is out of time you will have a defence to the claim but it is important that you mention it on your defence.

Is it a Small Claim?

Claims for the possession of land cannot be dealt with under the small claims procedure and Employment disputes such as claims for unfair dismissal and sexual or racial discrimination are dealt with by Industrial Tribunals.

Allocation to Another Track

Where a claim is referred for small claims track a district judge may order that it should not be treated as a small claim and there should be a trial in court instead if:

- The case raises a difficult question of law or a complex question of fact or

- Fraud is alleged against any party or

- The parties agree that the case should be tried in court or

- It would not be reasonable for the case to proceed as a small claim having regard to its subject matter, the size of any counterclaim and the circumstances of the parties or the interests of any other person likely to be affected by the award.

The judge can do this on his own initiative or in response to an application by any party.

Research your claim – or risk failure

In every case, it is important to research the legal basis for your claim until you are sure that you are on solid foundations before a claim form is issued. Poor preparation means a reduced chance of success while good preparation will boost your confidence and help you see it through to the end. You can seek advice at Law Centres, Citizens Advice Centres, some libraries will stock legal books, and most university law libraries will admit a member of the public. You are free to instruct a Solicitor to prepare your statement of case if your claim is complicated.

3

BRIEF NOTE ON OTHER TYPES OF CLAIM

Although not "small claims" the following information may be useful as it addresses situations that frequently arise. The brief description below is intended to let you know that the procedure exists and is available at your local county court. It is not intended to be a sufficient outline of the relevant law or procedure for you to proceed unaided so please take appropriate advice from a Solicitor or at the Citizens Advice Centre or Local Authority funded Law Centre before contemplating issuing a claim.

Consumer Credit Act 1974

Two forms of action are available to a creditor in difficulty:

- Time Order: the debtor can apply to the court for additional time to pay-off the credit

- If the interest on a loan is excessive, the debtor can apply to the court to re-open the agreement and decide a fairer rate of interest. An agreement that the court can re-open is known as an "Extortionate Credit Bargain"

Both may be brought as a counterclaim when a creditor issues proceedings under the CCA to enforce payment or recover goods. Legal advice should be obtained and it would be unwise to issue these claims without instructing a Solicitor.

Landlord & Tenant Act, 1954 – Business Tenancies

A business tenant has two important rights where the lease expires if the LTA 1954 has not been excluded at the beginning of the tenancy by a consent order, as follows

- The lessee can apply to the court for a new lease provided that certain notices and counter notices have or have not been served. The time limits for serving these notices are very strict and must be complied with.

- Compensation is payable by the Landlord to the tenant based upon the rateable value of the property in circumstances where the Landlord has proved a ground for possession

Assured Short Hold Tenancies: Claim for Possession
(Section 21 Housing Act, 1985)

The Landlord of a residential property let on an assured shorthold tenancy is entitled to end the tenancy by service of two months Notice to Quit (this is a statutory form) ending on a term date i.e. the fixed term date or a date when rent is paid.

The Notice to Quit must be for at least 2 months expiring on the fixed date for the end of the term, or on a periodic date where the tenancy has continued beyond the term date. The court may issue the order for possession without a hearing.

Administration Order: claim to reschedule debts

The courts with bankruptcy jurisdiction operate a procedure where a debtor with less that £5,000 outstanding can apply to the district judge to reduce the debts pro-rata and/or order overall payments by instalments. This is a useful means of avoiding bankruptcy where the level of indebtedness is relatively small. This procedure is explained further in chapter 14.

4

BEFORE LEGAL ACTION

Prevent claims Arising – Pre-emptive Action

It is highly desirable to avoid litigation if at all possible and the best way to do this is to prevent claims arising. There is nothing to be gained by issuing proceedings prematurely when there is scope to settle the claim without involving the court. The parties are under a general duty to negotiate and to settle the dispute without involving the court if at all possible.

If you are a consumer and intend to employ someone to perform a service obtain estimates beforehand outlining exactly what is to be done and how much it will cost. It is also wise to ask if the people you are doing business with belong to any professional or trade associations. Write and confirm all the details of the contract before the work begins. Disputes often result from oral contracts where neither party made a written record of what was agreed and understood by the parties at the time of the contract. Depending on the service you are buying, ensure that you have a written contract or that you use your standard terms of business in a sale or purchase.

If you run a business, problems occur if credit is extended to the wrong customer or is allowed to extend beyond a suitable amount. Do not extend credit without first obtaining trade references or limit credit to a small figure. Insist on payment before further credit is extended and establish a track record with the customer before being too relaxed about extending credit. The best advice in the case of a "can't pay, won't pay" customer is to issue proceedings sooner rather than later because if the claim is defended you could be out of pocket for up to three months due to the slowness of the courts If your business encounters serious problems in paying your creditors, negotiate terms of payment and discuss your situation openly and honestly. Such action at an early stage often avoids legal proceedings being taken against you. Always keep your bank manager informed and up to date with your business affairs and avoid giving him unexpected surprises.

Ensure that you keep all relevant documents, such as a receipt for a payment, the contract guarantees, delivery note or any letters written. Also keep a copy of any advertisement you relied on in entering into a contract. If you speak to anyone on the telephone, make a record of the person's name and of what was said. A case often turns on the documentary evidence available at the small claims track hearing and relevant documents with which you may have use to prove a case to the satisfaction of a judge usually come into existence before or during a dispute.

Steps you should take before issuing a claim form

Before issuing a claim form, make a clear complaint and attempt to reach a compromise by contacting the defendant. If no compromise or settlement is achieved, before issuing a claim form, you should write to the defendant threatening legal action and stating the recompense you are demanding. It is important to avoid issuing proceedings unnecessarily i.e. to write to the defendant with details of the claim before issuing proceedings. This is known as a "letter before action".

It is important to keep a copy of this and of all correspondence to produce at the court hearing.

Is the defendant a "man of straw"?

Before issuing a claim form to enforce a debt or payment of an invoice, etc, consider whether the defendant is worth suing. If he or she is completely penniless, you may live a longer and more contented life if you decided not to take legal action.

Pre-Action Protocols – Personal Injury

The new Rules have formally recognised that claims may be settled short of court action if there is a better exchange of information and more detailed investigation is undertaken before a claim is issued. The Rules provide for this by means of Pre-Action Protocols. The only Protocol relevant to small claim relates to personal injury. This Protocol set out the steps you should take in a personal injury action before issuing a claim form.

SAMPLE LETTERS BEFORE ACTION

Dear Mr. Cooke,

My tenancy in your flat at [address] ended on [date] and I duly moved out on that date. However I have still not received the repayment of my deposit of £   which under the terms of our lease agreement you should repay at the end of the tenancy. If I do not receive the money requested within fourteen days of receipt of this letter then I will have no option but to begin legal proceedings against you.

Yours sincerely,

J. Smith

Dear Mrs. Gibson,

The washing machine I purchased from you on [date] is not of satisfactory quality or fit for the purpose for which is was sold. It has torn a number of garments of a total value of £600. I have already visited your shop and made a complaint but I have received no response.

I wish to return the faulty machine, have the purchase price refunded and for you to pay me the cost of replacing my clothes. If I do not receive a satisfactory reply within fourteen days I will begin legal proceedings against you in the County Court.

Yours sincerely,

J. Smith

5

AN OVERVIEW OF

PROCEDURE

Part 7 governs the issue of the claim form. If a defence is not filed, judgement is entered for the claimant because the defendant is in default of the obligation to file a defence. If a defence is filed, the claim is in appropriate circumstances allocated to the small claims track and proceeds under the provisions of Part 27.

The procedure for small claims is informal. The district judge hears the case in a private room. You can claim fixed costs, your own personal costs, witness expenses up to £50 per day, and in certain cases expert fees for reports up to £260. Solicitors' fees are not awarded to the successful party. This is to encourage members of the public to conduct their own case. The small claims procedure is designed for lawyer-free self-representation.

The Court provides standard forms for completion by the opponents throughout a case with the intention that for simple matters, you could present your own case. The same forms are available from the Lord Chancellor's homepage.

Types of Small Claim

Your claim may be for a fixed amount or for an amount to be assessed. In the latter case, liability for the claim is treated separately from assessment of the amount of the claim. In such a case, you would write on the claim form e.g. "not more than £3,000" when the claim is for between £1.00 and £3,000. If a defence is not filed or if such a claim is admitted, you would obtain judgement with damages to be assessed by the district judge at a "disposal hearing". In most cases, you will know the amount of your claim.

Special Features of Part 7 Procedures

❑ The claimant is entitled to Judgement in default of the defendant filing the Acknowledgement of service and/or the defence, or

❑ Judgement on liability with damages to be assessed at a disposal hearing

Special features of the Small Claims Track

❑ Complicated rules do not apply

❑ The hearing is informal and not in open court

How To Start a Claim: Issue a Claim Form

The claim form is used to start proceedings in the County Court. This is a form that the claimant files in court. A claim form can be obtained from the Court Office or the Lord Chancellor's homepage. The "claim" is set out in a "Statement of Case". Part 16 states that the claim form must (a) contain a concise statement of the nature of the claim (b) specify the remedy which the claimant seeks (c) where the claimant seeks the payment of money, contain a statement of value and (d) contain such other matters as may be set out in a practice direction. The statement of value to qualify as a small claim must be a fixed money claim of £5,000 or below, and in the case of personal injury or a claim by a tenant against a landlord for £1,000 or less.

When you have completed the form two copies of the claim form must be taken to the Court Office and the Court Fee paid.

Response Pack

The court will then serve (i.e. post) the claim form on the defendant with a "Response Pack" containing four forms, a Form of Acknowledgement, a Form of Admission (N9A), a form for filing a Defence (N9B) and a form for filing a Counterclaim (N9B).

Admitted or Part Admitted Claims: Part 14

The DEFENDANT may either

- ❑ Admit/Part admit the claim with an offer to pay immediately. The court will enter judgement.

- ❑ Admit/Part Admit the claim with an offer to pay in instalments.

- ❑ If the claim is part admitted, a defence should be filed to show why part of the claim is not admitted

- ❑ If the claim is for an unspecified amount i.e. an amount to be assessed, the defendant can admit the claim and make an offer.

The CLAIMANT may then

- ❑ File an application for judgement of the admitted claim

- ❑ Accept or reject an offer of instalments on an admitted claim. If you reject the instalments offered, the court clerk will assess the defendant's statement of means and make an order for instalments. If you are dissatisfied with the clerk's decision, you may apply to the district judge for a determination.

❑ Reject a part admission; in which case the claim proceeds as if defended, and the defendant should file a defence.

❑ In the case of an admitted claim with the "amount to be assessed", you should apply for judgement to be entered for liability. The court will schedule a "disposal hearing" to determine the amount of the claim or damages payable. If an offer is made in respect of a claim for an unspecified sum, the offer may be either accepted or rejected. If it is rejected, the court will proceed to a "disposal hearing" for damages to be assessed

Refuted Claims

The defendant may as an alternative to admitting the claim:

❑ File the acknowledgement requesting 28 days to file the defence from date of service; or

❑ File a defence within 14 days; and/or

❑ File a counterclaim against the claimant; and/or

❑ Issue a Part 20 Notice against a non-party or a contribution notice against a co-defendant

Judgement in Default

If the defendant does not file a defence within 14 days of the date of service of the claim (or 28 days from the date of service of the claim if an acknowledgement of service has been filed), the court will at the request of the claimant order judgement in the claimant's favour without a hearing. This is judgement "in default" of the defendant filing a defence. The claimant should file a request for a default judgement after the time period has lapsed. If the amount of the claim is not specified on the claim form, then as indicated above, you should file the request and the court will order judgement for the claimant with damages to be assessed at a disposal hearing.

Defence

The defence is a statement of case and Part 16 requires that it states (a) which allegations in the particulars of claim are denied (b) which are not admitted or denied i.e. that the claimant must prove, and (c) which allegations are admitted. If an allegation is denied, the defendant must (a) state his reasons for denying it and (b) if he intends to put forward a different version of events, state his own version. A defendant who fails to address an allegation by denying it or offering a different version of events is taken to admit the allegation. If the defendant files a Defence, the Court will serve a copy on the claimant and the case will be transferred to the defendant's local or "home" court, which will process the claim along the small claims track. If you expect the defendant to file a defence, you will save time if you issue your claim form in his local County Court.

Counterclaim: Part 20

The defendant may make a counterclaim

❑   This will be heard with the claim. If it is for a sum greater than the claim, a court fee may be payable.

❑   If the counterclaim is above the small claims limit of £5,000 the district judge may allocate the claim to a different track.

The defendant's counterclaim is a claim made by the defendant against the claimant, which may be less than his claim, so his claim is reduced, or it may be greater. A counterclaim is a separate action and an alternative to the defendant issuing his own claim form. Both claims are therefore managed in one action or set of proceedings.

The defendant is in the same position as the claimant when making a counterclaim. The rules for the content of the counterclaim are the same as for any claim. The claimant must file a defence to the counterclaim to avoid judgement-in-default on the counterclaim. In this respect, the claimant is for the purposes of the counterclaim in the same position as a defendant and the rules governing the content of the defence apply.

Counterclaims are dealt with under Part 20. This Part also deals with claims by one defendant against another and circumstances in which a defendant wishes to issue proceedings against a non-party. If you as the defendant to a claim, or a defendant to a counterclaim, consider either to be applicable you should instruct a Solicitor.

Allocation to a Track: Allocation Questionnaire Form

If the defendant files a defence or counterclaim, the Court will:

- Post a form called an "Allocation Questionnaire" (N205A) to the parties. This form records the details of the claim, the case number and date of service. The case number is now the reference point for your case and no steps can be taken without quoting it

- Both parties must complete and file the Allocation Questionnaire. The claimant must pay £80 when filing this form.

Directions Issued by the Court

After the Allocation Questionnaire is received, or in default of filing the

Allocation Questionnaire, the court will allocate the claim to the small claims track and issue directions. These are the courts instructions as to how the case should proceed. District judges have wide powers to issue directions but for small claims PD27 provides standard form directions depending on the category of claim. The parties may apply for directions using form N244.

Enforcement Proceedings

If the defendant does not comply with a court order or judgement, you must take enforcement proceedings to enforce the judgement.

6

THE CLAIMANT – HOW TO COMPLETE THE CLAIM FORM

The Claim Form (N1)

The claim form has space for the names of the parties, brief details of the claim, the value (if a value statement is required), a box for the defendant's address, and box for amount claimed, court fee, solicitors costs (i.e. fixed costs are recoverable for a Solicitor to prepare the form), total amount and issue date. The back of the form is for Particulars of Claim, the statement of truth and claimants address.

The claim form requires the claimant's full name. If the claimant is a company give the address of the registered office. If it is a firm write "a firm" after the name. If you use a trade name write your name and then "trading as" followed by your business name.

Think carefully about whether you are the correct person in bringing the action. For example, if your spouse or a friend gave you a present that turn out to be aulty, and you want a refund of the purchase price, then the person who ctually bought the goods should be the claimant. Also consider whether you hould be suing a company rather than the individual you dealt with. Was the ndividual merely acting as the representative of the company rather than ealing with you in their own right? If you have a consumer credit or hire urchase agreement you should usually act against the finance company as well s the retailer.

he box in the left-hand corner is for the defendant's address and the laimant's address in inserted in the box in the same position on the reverse ide of the claim form. If the defendant is a company the address of its egistered office will be on its headed notepaper, or you can find it out by elephoning Companies House in Cardiff on 029 20380801.

Category of Claim

A brief description of what type of claim you are making is required in the next pace. This means stating what the claim consists of for example, breach of ontract, dishonoured cheque, non-payment of invoice or bad workmanship.

Statement of Case: Part 16

he particulars or details of your claim must be set out in the largest box on the everse side of the form, or on a separate piece of paper. The requirements of 'art 16/PD16 are set out in chapter 5.

t is important to use numbered paragraphs and to set out each point relevant to 'our case. For example in a claim for breach of contract, you should state the ollowing:

- That a contract was entered into with the defendant

- When it was made, was it written or oral, and if oral, the way in which it may be evidenced e.g. by reference to letters and documents

- The relevant terms of the contract including implied terms. For example terms implied by the sale of goods act

- That you have performed all or part of your side of the contract or why you have not done so

- That the contract has been breached and give details of what the defendant has done or failed to do that puts him in breach

- What damage you have suffered as a result of the defendant's breach of the contract and the term or provision that the defendant has not been complied with.

- And lastly, you must state what you claim; for example payment of an invoice (state the amount) and interest at the contractual or statutory rate.

If your claim is in tort such as personal injury rather than contract, for example you are alleging that the defendant was negligent, then you must state the following:

- Who the parties are (if relevant)

- Describe the accident or event which is the basis of your complaint and say when it took place

- That the accident or act you are complaining about was caused by the defendant's negligence or breach of duty and give details

- That you suffered damage as a result of the facts alleged and give details of all the damage

- And lastly, state what you are claiming by either stating the amount claimed, or that you would like damages to be assessed, and claim interest.

- Any claim for personal injury must comply with the Pre-Action Protocol.

You should then sign the statement of truth and file two at the court. Keep a copy for your records.

Practice Direction 16

PD 16 identifies specific matters that must be addressed in the particulars of claim for personal injury, fatal accident claims, claims for the recovery of land, and hire purchase claims. In particular, if relevant, the written contract or relevant conditions of sale should be attached to the claim form. Where the claim is based on an oral contract, the particulars of claim should state the contractual words used, who said these words, where and when they were said. If the contract is to be proved by conduct or a course of dealing, the particulars must state the conduct or acts relied upon and by whom, when and where the acts constituting the conduct was done.

Duty to Mitigate

The claimant is under a positive duty to take steps to minimise or reduce the loss suffered as a result of the defendants' breach of contract or breach of duty. The claim should be for the loss suffered after mitigation.

Statement of Truth

Each statement of case and witness statement must be endorsed with a signed Statement of Truth. A false statement that is verified by a statement of truth is a contempt of court and penalties for contempt would apply if the judge took the matter further.

Claim for Interest

An interest claim may be made under the terms of a contract where specific provision is made or under statute. The County Court Act 1981 allows interest to be claimed from the date of the Act or breach that gave rise to the claim to the date of judgement. The Lord Chancellor determines the rate of interest and the court will know the current rate.

The claim will therefore be "for interest pursuant to the County Court Act 1981 section 69 from W date to X date at the rate of [8%] being a total of £Y and thereafter at the daily rate of £Z from the date of issue to the date of judgement or sooner payment" when W is the date of the breach and X is the date of issue of the claim form. Interest is payable on judgements in excess of £5,000 after judgement until payment.

When the claim is for damages to be assessed by the court, the claim will be "for interest pursuant to the County Court Act 1981 section 69 from W date to X date at the rate of [8%] and thereafter at the rate of [8%] to the date of judgement until sooner payment as the court shall determine to be just". It is not possible to calculate the interest to issue or the daily rate without knowing the level of damages awarded.

What to do Next

Take the two copies of the completed claim form to the court and pay the issue fee. Remember to keep a copy for yourself. The court may ask for copies. The court will stamp the claim form and post it to the defendant with forms of admission, defence and counterclaim, explained in the next chapter. The defendant must reply to your claim form within 14 days from the date of service printed on the Allocation Questionnaire. If the defendant files a defence, the court will post a copy to you. A form of Admission is returned direct to the claimant.

Accepting an Admission & Offer of Payment

As explained in the next chapter, the court serves a claim form on the defendant with a form of Admission Defence and Counterclaim. If the defendant admits the claim, the form of admission is posted direct to you, the claimant. You must then complete and return it to the court requesting judgement and an order for payment. You may request judgement but object to the method of payment, or accept a part admission but pursue the balance in respect of which the defendant should file a defence and/or counterclaim.

If the defendant admits the claim but asks for time to pay, you may reject the proposal. In the event of a dispute, the court staff will set an amount with reference to the information supplied by the defendant. The order to pay is issued on form N30(2), but if you object to the level of instalments, you are entitled to make an application to the district judge using form N244 for him to set a level of instalments. The case is then transferred to the defendant's local court for a hearing.

7

THE DEFENDANT – HOW TO RESPOND

This chapter examines the position of a defendant. The court serves the claim form on the defendant with the Response Pack containing forms for Admission, Defence and Counterclaim. The claimant is also a defendant when a counterclaim has been filed. The counterclaim is equivalent to a claim and the claimant must file a defence to the counterclaim or judgement in default would be available to the defendant/claimant. The effect of filing a defence is that the court will post Allocation Questionnaire forms to both parties. When the Allocation Questionnaires are returned, the claim will be allocated to the small claims track, directions will be issued, and a hearing will be arranged.

Judgement in Default of a Defence

If a judgement debt is not paid, a record is maintained on the Register of County Court Judgements for six years. This register is open to credit reference agencies. If judgement in default is entered against you, then you must either

- Apply for it to be set aside, or

- Pay the sum demanded, and/or

- Apply to pay by instalments

Admit, Defend and/or Counterclaim

If you do not admit the claim or file a defence, and/or counterclaim, the court will then enter "judgement-in-default" against you at the request of the claimant. This means that the court will order you to either:

- Pay the sum demanded, or

- In the case of an unspecified sum, judgement will be entered against you with damages to be assessed at a disposal hearing.

Form of Admission

The effect of an admission is that the claimant will be entitled to judgement in respect of the amount you admit. The issue then is the method of payment and whether the claimant or the court will permit payment by instalments. It is possible just to admit part of the claim if you believe that the claimant is not entitled to the whole amount but in such a case, you must use the forms of defence and/or counterclaim to deny that you owe the balance of the claim. If an admission is filed but the claimant does not accept your offer to pay by instalments, the court staff will set an amount with reference to the information you supply. If you object to the level of instalments ordered by the court staff, you are entitled to make an application for the district judge to assess the level of instalments.

The Form of Defence

If you deny that the claimant's claim is valid you must file a defence. However you can only file a defence if you have a reason for disputing the claimant's claim and not just a reluctance to pay him. Examples are that work done was faulty, the wrong goods were supplied and that the debt is really owed to another person. You should also file a defence if you admit part of the claim and the claimant will not accept your offer of part payment in full settlement. You must say why you do not owe the full amount.

Preparing the Defence

The defence must answer every claim made in the statement of case and make allegations on behalf of the defendant. In essence, each claim must be admitted or denied. Use numbered paragraphs if at all possible, unless the defence is simple. Look very carefully at the claimant's claims. Go through the statement of case methodically and try to respond to every allegation by denying it, admitting it or saying that you do not know. If you deny something then the claimant must prove the allegation. If you admit something it means that the claimant does not have to prove that particular point and the court will take it as accepted. It is important to also put forward your side of the story summarising what really happened and why it means you are not liable to the claimant as the claims. However, remember that if you are making a claim of your own against the claimant, then the allegations that relate to this should be made in the counterclaim and not in the defence.

As well as putting forward an alternative version or interpretation of events you can also take issue with the amount of damage the claimant claims to have suffered. For example, you might say that goods, which were damaged, are not as valuable as the claimant claims or his injury was not as serious as the claimant suggests.

You are also entitled to expect a claimant to mitigate these losses. This means that the claimant must take all reasonable steps to minimise the loss suffered even if the defendant was at fault.

The claimant is not entitled to recover damages that the defendant can prove resulted from a failure to mitigate. If you are unsuccessful in your defence, the court will order you to pay the full amount the claimant is seeking.

The Form of Counterclaim – Part 20

If you wish to make a claim against the claimant, you may file a counterclaim. This is equivalent to issuing your own claim form against the claimant. The counterclaim is a separate action that will be considered with the original claim. As with a claimant's original claim, you must request either a fixed amount or damages to be assessed. If the counterclaim is in excess of the small claims limit this does not prevent the case being automatically referred to small claims track but it is one of the factors a district judge can take into account when considering whether the case should be allocated to the small claims track. A court fee will be payable if the counterclaim exceeds the claim against you.

The counterclaim should be particularised using numbered paragraphs that state clearly what you claim, why the claimant is liable and what compensation you require. The claimant should file a defence to your counterclaim or you will be entitled to judgement in default.

Setting Aside a Default Judgement

If a Default Judgement is made against you when you have a "real prospect of successfully defending the claim", the court has a discretion to set aside a default judgement. You may apply to the Court for the judgement to be set aside by using form N244. Your application must be supported by evidence i.e. a witness statement verified by a statement of truth. You must give reasons for your failure to file a defence and convince the judge that your defence is genuine. The court must have regard to whether the application was made promptly, and conditions may be imposed on allowing you to defend e.g. that a defence is filed within 14 days. Delay in making the application after the judgement in default is received could be fatal to its success. In practice, the proposed defence should be attached to the witness statement filed in support of the application, or at the very least, the witness statement should set out what the defence is available to the defendant.

Transfer to the Defendant's "home court"

The application to set aside or the claim itself will be heard at the defendant's local court unless the claimant can give good reasons why it should not be transferred.

Claims against Others – Part 20

A defendant who holds a third party entirely or partly responsible for the claimant's loss is entitled to join the third party in the action by issuing a Part 20 Notice. Leave of the court is required to issue the Notice if the defence has been filed.

An example of where you might want to join a third party is if the claimant brings an action seeking compensation for damage to his car caused by you driving into the back of it. But you only hit the claimant's vehicle because your car was shunted forward as a result of being hit by a third party's car. In such circumstances you would want the third party to be joined in the action as he is the person who is really responsible for the damage.

8

SETTLING THE DISPUTE

It may be worth your while to try and reach a compromise with your opponent and to settle the case without a small claims track hearing. This is because all litigation contains some element of risk. However much you believe in your own case there is almost always a chance that the district judge's decision could go against you. By reaching a settlement you save yourself the risk of losing completely in return for conceding something to your opponent. You also save yourself the time and trouble involved in arguing the merits of the case in front of the district judge. Think carefully about the strengths and weaknesses of your case, and then decide what you would be prepared to accept. It is important to be realistic. Any counterclaim should be settled at the same time.

How to Negotiate a Settlement

If you want to reach a settlement you can write to your opponent and make them an offer. Letters concerning settlements are usually headed "without prejudice". The practical effect of heading your letter "without prejudice" is that if your opponent refuses your offer or ignores it, then the letter and its contents cannot be used as evidence against you. This means you can make admissions in without prejudice correspondence and "horse trade" without fear that your concessions will not count against you. The letter before action should not be without prejudice and it should make a claim at the highest level you consider your claim is worth. If the offer is accepted after without prejudice correspondence, it should be agreed in open correspondence to become a binding agreement to settle the action.

You could also write to your opponent and ask if he would be prepared to discuss the case on the telephone or arrange a meeting in the hope that you can negotiate a settlement. If you do not know your opponent well exercise caution if the dispute is heated.

When entering into negotiations it is important to be prepared. It is a good idea to write down three figures in advance. Firstly, an opening offer or request which might be slightly more than you expect to receive or less than you expect to pay, secondly the figure you would be happy to accept or to pay and thirdly your bottom line which is the minimum you would accept or the maximum you would pay your opponent. It is particularly important to decide on the final figure and keep it in mind so that an aggressive opponent cannot push you into an unfavourable settlement.

When to Negotiate

You are free to negotiate at any time, from before the start of legal proceedings until the district judge makes his judgement. In small claims the disclosure of evidence normally takes place only one or two weeks before the date set for small claims track. If you feel that seeing your opponent's documents and expert's reports is likely to effect your view of the strength or weakness of their case it may be worth waiting until you have received copies before reaching any agreement.

When to Accept an Offer

If your opponent makes you an offer of settlement consider what his motives may be. If it is very low it could be that he has misjudged the strength of his own case but alternatively he may have spotted a genuine weakness in your case that you have not noticed. You are free to ask him why he thinks that amount is reasonable. If the offer is high you will naturally want to come to a decision quickly in case it is withdrawn but you should not necessarily accept it immediately. There may be a weakness in his case you do not yet know about or yours might be stronger than you think. If a relatively large sum is involved it might be worth taking advice on whether or not to accept it.

Consent Orders

The Court will normally approve a settlement that both sides accept. This is achieved by a consent order. A formal form of consent may be signed and filed with the Court any time before the hearing. The parties are under a general duty to attempt a negotiated settlement and to inform the court if agreement is achieved in advance of the hearing. The court would obviously prefer to save time and deal with the consent order by post. Both sides should write to the court outlining their agreement; or for one party to set out the agreed compromise and the other to sign at the foot of the letter. The judge must approve a consent order before or at the hearing. At the hearing, if a compromise were agreed, the judge would record the agreement and the court draws up a consent order or judgement.

Withdrawing the Claim Form

If a settlement has been agreed, the claimant may file a Notice of Discontinuance (Form N297) and a certificate saying that the defendant has been informed of withdrawal of the claim form. The case would be ended without a court order. This option may be suitable if the claimant simply abandons the case altogether, or if the defendant pays an agreed sum in one payment. If instalments are agreed, the claimant is better off with a court order that is capable of enforcement. A consent order would be preferable to a discontinuance.

9

PREPARING FOR THE SMALL CLAIMS TRACK HEARING

Preliminary Appointments

The court controls what steps should be taken before the hearing by issuing "directions". The usual directions for a small claims track case are listed in Practise Direction 27. Either party can make an application to the court on form N244 for a preliminary appointment at which the party may request additional directions. You may wish to apply for additional directions if the standard directions do not cover all the points. Your main concern will be directions concerning evidence, and disclosure of evidence such as documents, or for permission to produce photographs.

This is not usually necessary in small claims proceedings to require non-standard directions. The other party may oppose your application or not attend the hearing. If at all possible, try and agree the directions with your opponent then both parties can write to the court asking for the same direction. In nearly all cases, the court will grant any directions which both parties request.

A preliminary appointment is informal and takes place in a private room with a district judge and the litigants present. Remember, a preliminary appointment is not the small claims track. Beyond establishing whether or not you have an arguable claim or defence the judge will not consider the merits of the case at this stage so you do not need to take along witnesses or to be fully prepared to argue your case at this point.

Applications Generally – Form 244

An application used to require a hearing. Under the new rules, form 244 allows the applicant to indicate that he wishes the judge to deal with the application without a hearing. If the subject matter of the application is contentious or disputed, it is safer to request a hearing. Preliminary applications attract a court fee of £50. All applications must be supported by evidence i.e. a witness statement.

Failure to Attend a Preliminary Appointment

The district judge may order a preliminary appointment. If the claimant fails to attend despite the judges order, the judge will probably strike the case out. If the defendant does not attend, the judge could either issue direction, strike out the defence, or if the admission is filed, allow the claimant to prove the level of loss suffered.

Trial Date & Time Estimates

If it has not done so already the court will set a date for the small claims track. If you cannot attend on the date set inform the court immediately. The judge who issues the directions will give a time estimate of how long he expects the case to last. If the time estimate is too short, write to the court and/or telephone the listings clerk because otherwise the judge may not have time to hear your case in full and you will have to go back on another date. Another appointment is unlikely to be immediately available so this will mean you have to wait longer to get the case resolved. Either the claimant or the defendant can ask for more time. Allow plenty of time for your witnesses to give their evidence and to be questioned by your opponent.

Complying with Directions

It is essential that you comply with the district judge's directions concerning what should be done and exchanged before the trial. Failure to exchange documentary evidence and expert reports may mean that you cannot use such evidence during the small claims track hearing and this could seriously harm your prospects of success.

Your Own Preparations for the Small Claims Track

Although small claims hearings are informal, many people feel apprehensive at the prospect of presenting their case to the district judge. The better you prepare before the hearing the more confident you will be when you attend the small claims track. Remember that you are a witness in your own case and that the issues are defined in your statement of case and the defence. In general, there is a conflict in the evidence and the district judge will be deciding whose evidence he finds most credible. The strict procedure is that the claimant makes a case and the defendant then presents a defence, as follows:

- The claimant. You will have to be prepared to introduce the case to the district judge by telling him what it is about, what happened, why the defendant was at fault and what is at issue or in dispute. It is a good idea to write a list of important points in the order you want to mention them so that you do not forget things or repeat yourself. Look back at your particulars of claim and the defence to make sure you have not overlooked anything. If you can, find an obliging friend, practice explaining your case and ask them if what you say is clear and easy to follow.

- The defendant. You will have to respond to the claimant's claims or rebut his allegations. However, you will know in advance what claims have been made, so you will be able to predict much of what the claimant will say. Look at the particulars of claim and the documents you receive from the claimant such as expert's reports. Make your own note of the key allegations being made against you and then be prepared to outline your defence to the district judge rebutting each of these allegations. Make a list of the points you intend to make in order. You may benefit from practice in explaining your defence to a friend or relative.

- Preparing to deal with witnesses. Once you have outlined your claim or defence you will have the opportunity to call witnesses to give evidence. Before the small claims track reflect on why you are calling each witness and what you hope they will say that will strengthen your case or weaken your opponents. Prepare a few questions with which you could prompt them to discuss the relevant matter without actually giving the court the evidence yourself. For example: "What did you see after the red car came around the corner of Smith Street?" is preferable to "The defendant drove around the corner of Smith Street too fast, swerved all over the road and then negligently drove over my bicycle, didn't he?" The district judge will have already heard your account of events; he now wants to hear from the witness. You may undermine the strength of his evidence if you, in effect, tell him what to say. Preparing questions in advance will help you to resist the natural temptation to try and give the witness's evidence for him. You will also get an opportunity to question your opponent's witnesses, this is known as cross-examination. When doing this the recommendation about not giving evidence for them does not apply, in that you can make a statement of fact such as "the defendant was going too fast wasn't he?" or "the claimant had left his bicycle in the middle of the road hadn't he?" and ask them for a yes or no answer. Try to think in advance of anything, which weakens or discredits their evidence. For example that they could not have had a very good view of the accident, they are in business with your opponent, or their memory of events is imperfect on one point so should not be relied on in relation to another question.

- In general when you are preparing for the hearing it is a good idea to try and step back from the case. This is difficult as you will naturally feel strongly about your claim or defence but if you can try and see it from an impartial viewpoint and then try and think from your opponent's perspective you may get a clearer appreciation of the strengths and weaknesses of your case and be better able to predict what will be raised at the small claims track.

- In preparation for the hearing have plenty of copies of the documents with you because you may have to supply them to the district judge or your opponent and photocopying at court costs £1 for every sheet.

It could also be worth your while trying to reach agreement with your opponent before the small claims track hearing.

Witness statements

The most basic standard directions (Form A attached to Practice Direction 27) do not require witness statements to be prepared. This simply requires that all documents be exchanged with copies filed in court and the originals to be brought to the hearing. It is open to you, nevertheless, to prepare and file a witness statement voluntarily. This practice would give the court advanced notice of your case beyond the statement of case, and the documents and/or photographs you rely on can be attached to the witness statement and referred to. Your evidence should be written and any other witnesses should file witness statements with copies served on the defendant. This will help you present your case at the hearing if you can refer to your statement when issues arise.

10

EVIDENCE

Our legal system is in principle adversarial and not inquisitorial. This means that both parties to a dispute must present a case to a judge who acts as an impartial observer. The small claims procedure is an exception to this rule in that the judge will be more involved. He will ask questions and try and find out what he needs to know. Nevertheless it is the responsibility of the parties to supply the evidence for the judge to consider.

Types of Evidence

Evidence is factual information that can be presented to the court to enable the judge to decide on the probability of a claim that has been made being correct or true. In all cases, the claimant and the defendant are witnesses in their own case. The claims made in the particulars of claim or in a defence or any other statement of case must be proven with evidence. Evidence can take a number of different forms:

- Oral Evidence. Both the claimant and the defendant will be able to give evidence by speaking to the district judge, giving their account of events and presenting their arguments. They can also call witnesses to attend court and give oral evidence about any relevant fact of which they have knowledge. If a witness is unwilling to attend the hearing, you are entitled to compel their attendance by issuing a witness form

(Form N20). This must be done at least seven days before the hearing, and it will mean that you have to pay the witnesses' expenses and the cost of their travel to and from the court. Court staff will tell you how much this is. If you are successful and win the case you should be able to recover the cost of the witnesses travelling and overnight expenses reasonably incurred and £50 for their loss of earnings from your opponent.

- Witness Statements. In general, the oral evidence should be supported by witness statements, filed in court and served on the other party. This is not one of the standard directions and therefore not a strict requirement but it is a good tactic to prepare and serve witness statements regardless of the directions made by the court. Witnesses who are unable to attend the hearing can give their evidence in writing. They should give their full name and address and sign and date their statement. Such evidence can be very useful but, depending on the circumstances, it is likely to carry less weight than direct oral testimony because the other party and the judge do not have the opportunity to question the witness, and because seeing someone give their evidence would help the district judge to decide how credible he finds that witness. On the other hand, if you get your witness to make a statement prior to the hearing and ask your opponent if they will accept that the evidence contained in the statement is correct you may be able to save the cost and trouble of bringing the witness to court. Witness statements are also useful where you have a number of witnesses who are going to say the same thing. You can ask one of them to attend the hearing and request that the others make statements. Photocopies of witness statements should be given to the other party prior to the hearing in accordance with the court's directions.

• Photographs & Documentary Evidence. This includes things like contracts, letters, a returned cheque, estimates, delivery notes, receipts, diary entries, guarantees and photographs. Judges are usually faced with parties giving contradictory oral evidence and the difficult job of choosing between them, so documentary evidence which supports one account rather than the other is very helpful. It is often a good idea to take photographs in preparation for the case. For example if you are making a claim against a builder who you say has done bad work or you have been physically injured then having a photograph of things like the bad work, the injury and the scene of the accident will not only improve your credibility but may also help the judge to form a clearer picture of what went on and what is at issue. You can also use or draw up plans or maps to help you explain what happened. This is particularly useful in disputes about road accidents. It may save time if you can get your opponent to agree in writing before the hearing that your plans are accurate.

Other Physical Evidence & Site Visits. In addition to documents you can use other physical evidence to support your claims. For example if the dispute is about reasonably small and portable goods you could take the goods in question, or a sample, along to the small claims track to show that they are faulty in some way. In some circumstances the district judge may want to visit the scene of the accident or the place where unsatisfactory work was done, or to go and see an object which cannot be brought to the court. This is known as a site visit and both the claimant and the defendant will be given notice in advance and the opportunity to attend.

- <u>Expert Evidence</u> may be filed with the courts permission. This is required when it is necessary to decide a question that requires specialist or technical knowledge that the district judge is unlikely to have. For example, a surveyor may give an opinion on building works and a doctor will be a suitable expert in personal injury cases. When a matter calls for expert evidence only a suitably qualified person can give it. This does not necessarily mean that they must have formal qualifications although these are usually expected and it may be difficult to satisfy a judge that a witness is an expert if he does not have formal qualifications. You will see in chapter 15 that if you win the case, you can claim from the defendant (or the claimant) up to £260 for the cost of an expert report.

- To find an expert you can contact the relevant professional or trade association and ask for a recommendation or a Citizens Advice Bureau or Trading Standards Officer may be able to help you find a suitable person. It is important not to use an expert you already have close connections with such as a relative or friend because the district judge is likely to give less weight to the evidence of an expert who is not entirely independent.

- When you have found a suitable expert ask him to write a report. Explain clearly what you want and what is at issue. This will ensure he answers the important questions and also that he does not do unnecessary work which will increase your costs. It may be possible for both you and your opponent to minimise your expenses by agreeing to use the same expert. In which case you should agree in advance what questions you want the expert to answer and what evidence he will see. Another alternative is for you to ask the court to appoint an expert to act as the district judge in place of the district judge. In such circumstances you and your opponent would share the costs. If you already have a pre-small claims track appointment you can request that the district judge agree to this procedure at that hearing. Alternatively you can apply on Form N244 and you will be given an appointment.

- Remember that you must obtain the courts permission to present expert evidence, by completing the relevant part of the questionnaire or by letter. Also remember to give copies of expert reports to your opponent and to the court before the small claims track date in accordance with the courts directions.

SPECIAL CASES – Road Traffic Accidents, Personal Injury; etc

The small claims track is available to minor personal injuries and claims of a more complex nature than a simple money claim. This is not an invitation to take on more than you understand and in appropriate circumstances you should take advice before rushing in with an ill-prepared claim. A more difficult case would obviously require a more detailed understanding of the evidence required to succeed.

The Burden of Proof

It is the claimant who brings the case to court and who makes allegations about the defendant or his conduct and it is for the claimant to establish that these claims are true. In legal terms it is said that he bears the burden of proof.

Although the claimant formally bears the burden of proof, on a practical level both the claimant and the defendant can be subject to the "onus of proof". This means that when the claimant has made a plausible allegation and substantiated his claims, for example producing evidence that goods were delivered but not paid for then the onus is on the defendant to give an answer or give an explanation. The defendant might produce evidence of payment. This would then put the onus of proof back on the claimant. The claimant could allege that the payments were for other invoices and so on.

Because the claimant bears the burden of proof, if at the end of the hearing the district judge finds that the claimant's and the defendant's arguments are of equal strength he must decide in favour of the defendant and dismiss the claim form. When he is making a counterclaim the defendant bears the burden of proof in respect of this part of the case.

The Standard of Proof

It is unlikely that either party will be able to prove their case with 100% certainty but this is not required. In order to discharge the burden of proof the claimant (or in a counterclaim the defendant) must show he is right "on the balance of probabilities". This means that the district judge must be satisfied that what he is claiming is more likely than not to be correct. The criminal standard of proof that a case must be proved "beyond reasonable doubt" does not normally have any application in small claims.

What You Must Prove

At the hearing the claimant must prove each of the statements made in his particulars of claim, which amount to establishing liability, and the level of loss suffered; because if he is successful, the court will award damages to compensate him for his loss, not to punish the defendant. The claimant does not have to prove any of the particulars that are admitted by the defendant in his defence. It is also the claimant's responsibility to prove that the defendant received the claim form. This is relevant when the defendant does not attend the hearing or attends but denies service, but it is not relevant when the defendant has returned one of the forms of admission, defence and counterclaim. The court will normally assume due service if the claim form is not returned by the post office.

Likewise, the defendant must prove all of the allegations he makes in the counterclaim and the level of loss he may have suffered. He should also bring any evidence available to him which disproves or undermines any of the claimant's claims in the particulars of claim, including those about the extent of the loss he has suffered, or which supports the defendant's alternative account of events.

The Rules of Evidence

The rules of evidence that normally govern what evidence is admissible, which means what the judge will consider and take into account, do not apply to small claims.

11

REPRESENTATION

The small claims procedure is designed with the intention that people will be able to conduct their own case and legal representation should not usually be necessary. Consequently you are allowed to have a lay representative to state your case for you, perhaps a friend or relative who feels more confident about speaking to the judge. A lay representative cannot be heard if the person he represents does not attend the hearing and the district judge has the right to exclude him for misconduct. A limited company may be represented by a director.

Parties to a small claim are also entitled to employ a solicitor if they wish. However they will be unable to recover the cost of legal representation from their opponent if they are successful and so they will have to pay the costs themselves. Legal aid is not normally available for representation in small claims. If a party is unable to properly represent themselves in a small claim, for example as a result of a physical disability, poor sight, pronounced stammer or inability to read, these circumstances can be taken into account by the district judge when deciding whether or not the case should be automatically referred to small claims track or whether it should go to a county court trial for which legal aid may be available.

If you feel you are unable to represent yourself inform the court well before the small claims track date and ask for a preliminary appointment for directions.

You could also apply for legal aid on the grounds that your circumstances are exceptional.

You may feel that your opponent is a better advocate or has instructed a solicitor. Inequality of representation can be worrying. However, the district judge will take a fairly active role to ensure that you are not unfairly disadvantaged. The district judge will be mindful of the overriding objective and the duty of the court to "deal with cases justly" and to "ensure that the parties are on an equal footing".

12

SMALL CLAIMS TRACK AND JUDGMENT

You will receive notification of the date, time and place set for the small claims track hearing from the court when the case has been allocated to the small claims track. If you have not been there before allow plenty of time to find the court. You may wear what you wish but it is a good idea to dress smartly to make a favourable impression on the district judge. Bring the originals and spare copies of all the documents and the evidence you want to use at the hearing even though you have already sent copies to the court and your opponent.

When you arrive at court you will find a list of the days cases on a notice board. Check that your case is listed and inform the usher that you have arrived. The usher will know if your opponent has arrived, and if he is represented by a solicitor.

Unless you have a relatively long time estimate such as a full day, cases are usually listed in blocks. For example, a number of cases will be listed for 10.00 a.m. and 2.00 p.m. and will be heard in order. This means you are likely to have to spend some time waiting around before the hearing. This gives you an opportunity to check that your opponent has received all the documents you or the court have served on him, and if he has not let him have a look at a copy. The waiting period could also give you an opportunity to settle the dispute if you consider it worthwhile, but beware of accepting an unfavourable settlement because of pre-hearing nerves. If you do achieve a compromise the judge will most likely approve it at the hearing and issue a consent order.

When it is your turn to be heard the usher will show you into the judge's room. The judge will usually be sitting at the end of a long table. You and your opponent will sit on either side. The judge will not be wearing a wig or gown and should be addressed as "Sir or Madam". Ask the judge if he would prefer the witnesses to wait outside and be called in when required, or if they may sit in on the full hearing. Only the people involved in the case will be present. Evidence is not given on oath unless the district judge directs that it should be.

Because it is the claimant who has brought the case to the small claims track and it is the claimant who has made allegations or claims against the defendant it is usual for the claimant to begin by presenting his case at the hearing. The defendant will then have an opportunity to respond.

How to Present Your Case – The claimant

- Ask the judge if he or she has all the documents in the case such as the claim form, defence, expert's reports and witness statements. If you have filed a witness statement ask the judge to read it.

- Take the judge through the list of points you have prepared or the particulars of claim to explain your case. Identify what the defendant has admitted in the defence. This should give the judge a clear idea of what is at issue and thus what he is being asked to decide.

- Having given an outline of your case, introduce the evidence you have to support it. This may include your own oral evidence, documents and possibly witnesses, although this is not essential.

- You, the judge and your opponent will all have an opportunity to question your witnesses. You will also be able to question your opponent and his witnesses.

- Except when you are questioning witnesses you should address your remarks to the judge. Avoid getting involved in any direct argument with your opponent.

- Your may feel more confident in presenting your case if you have prepared and filed a witness statement yourself. You could then refer to your own statement when speaking to the district judge or answering questions

How to Present Your Case – The defendant

- You will probably have to wait while the claimant presents his claims against you to the judge. This may be very frustrating but do not interrupt or speak over your opponent. You will have an opportunity to put your side of the story later on.

- When the claimant is speaking make a note of any important points he makes. For example if there is something you would like to question him about later or a fact that has not emerged previously.

- After the claimant has spoken you will have the opportunity to present your defence. Use the notes you have prepared or your defence form to help you as you tell the judge all the important points.

- Try to respond to what the claimant has said.

- You will have an opportunity to call your witnesses and question them as well as an opportunity to question your opponent and his witnesses.

- If you have filed a Counterclaim this must be presented as though you were a claimant.

- Your may feel more confident in presenting your case if you have prepared and filed a witness statement yourself. You could then refer to your own statement when speaking to the district judge or answering questions

Whether you are a claimant or a defendant it is in your own best interests to remain calm and courteous throughout the hearing.

Small Claims are Informal

The description outlined above makes the hearing seem rather formal. In practice, the judge may intervene and ask questions and the hearing will "ebb and flow" as the judge seeks to extract relevant information from both sides.

As the hearing may move on quickly, it is important to be familiar with the detail of your claim or defence and to "put the record straight" when any detail is ignored or misunderstood.

Failure to Attend

If the claimant fails to attend, the judge could decide that there is no case to answer and dismiss the claim form.

In such a case, the claimant could apply for judgement to be set aside if grounds exist. If the defendant fails to attend, the judge could enter judgement for the claimant or decide that there is no case to answer and dismiss the claim form.

If you find you are going to be unable to attend contact the court immediately to seek an adjournment.

Judgement

If a compromise is not possible, the judge will decide on the evidence whether the claimant has proved the case and is entitled to the orders requested. The judge will usually make a decision on the claim and counterclaim (if any) at the hearing. Be careful to write down what the judgement is and all the relevant detail. The court will prepare the form of judgement and serve it on both sides. If it is inaccurate or incorrect, contact the court immediately.

13

ENFORCING THE
JUDGMENT

In this chapter the judgement debtor is referred to as the defendant but judgement debtors can also be claimants who have lost a counterclaim. Once you have obtained judgement on the claim or counterclaim no further action is required so long as the damages are paid. However judgement debtors do not always comply with the court's order to pay a lump sum and may fall into arrears with payments to be made by instalments, in which case you have a number of options and can ask the court for any of the following:

A Warrant of Execution

This gives a bailiff the authority to visit the defendant's home or business and try to collect the money you are owed or to take goods to sell at auction. You can ask the bailiff to recover the whole amount or alternatively you can ask for part of the debt for example one or more instalments, or a minimum of £50.

You cannot normally ask for a part warrant if you originally asked for the judgement to be paid in one amount. A fee will be charged and this will be added to the amount you are owed by the defendant. The fee will not be refunded if the bailiff is not able to get anything from the defendant.

To request a warrant of execution, fill in form N323 and send it to the court. If you would like confirmation that the warrant has been issued you must also enclose a stamped addressed envelope. The court will send the defendant a notice to let him know that a warrant has been issued and that he must pay what is owed within seven days. If he complies the court will send the moneys on to you. If he does not the bailiff will call at his address within 15 working days of the warrant being issued to collect payment or take goods. The cost of taking and selling such goods will be deducted from the amount they raise when they are sold and then you will be sent your money.

There are limits placed on the type of goods a bailiff may take. He cannot take any items which are necessary for the basic domestic needs of the defendant and his family such as clothing or bedding or any items he requires to do his job or carry on his trade such as tools and vehicles. All property seized must belong to the defendant which means the bailiff cannot take goods which the defendant has on hire purchase, lease or which are rented, or which belong to someone else, such as the defendant's spouse. The bailiff may only take goods likely to fetch money at auction.

The bailiff is not entitled to break into the defendant's house to remove property. He may only enter with permission, however he may be able to break into the defendant's business premises if no one is living there.

The defendant is entitled to ask that the warrant be suspended, in which case you will have a number of options. You can agree to the suspension of the warrant and accept the defendant's offer of payment, or agree to the suspension and ask that he pay more than the amount he has suggested. This would mean that a court officer would decide how much the defendant can afford to pay.

Finally you can say that you do not agree to the suspension of the warrant and a hearing will be arranged.

If you object to the court officers decision about how much the defendant should pay fill in form N244 saying why you object and return it within sixteen days of the date of the postmark shown on the envelope the new order came in. A hearing will be arranged where a district judge will decide what the defendant should pay.

If the warrant is suspended but the defendant still does not pay you can use form N445 to ask the court to reissue the warrant. There is no fee for doing this. If the bailiff was unable to recover any money or goods from the defendant and you have further information which means you think he should be able to then you can also reissue the warrant in these circumstances. For example, if you have a new address for the defendant or you can give details of an item the defendant owns and which would be worth selling use form N445 to inform the court.

A warrant lasts for one year. If you have still not received payment near the end of that time you should apply to extend the life of the warrant before the year ends otherwise you will have to ask for another warrant and a fee will be charged.

An Attachment of Earnings Order

If the defendant is in employment, he still owes you over £50 and he is behind with his payments you may be able to get an attachment of earnings order against him. This means the court will receive payments direct from the defendants employer either monthly or weekly, depending on how he is paid and then will pass the money on to you.

To request an attachment of earnings order fill in form N55 and send it to the office of the defendant's local court with the fee. If your judgement was obtained in another court you should first write to that original court, explain that you want an attachment of earnings order and ask that the case be transferred. The defendant's local court will give you a new case number and you can then send in the request form N55 and the fee. Enclose a stamped addressed envelope if you would like confirmation that your request is being dealt with.

The court will tell the defendant to pay the money owed or to fill in a form giving details of his income, expenditure and employment. A court officer will then decide how much the defendant can afford to pay having made allowance for what he needs to live on. The order will then be sent to the defendant's employer telling him what and when he should pay.

If you are not happy with the court officer's decision you can use form N244 to ask for a district judge to decide what the defendant can afford to pay. You must say why you object to the decision and return the form within sixteen days of the date of the postmark shown on the envelope which the attachment of earnings order came in. A hearing will then be arranged.

The defendant is entitled to ask that the order should be suspended and that he should be allowed to make payments directly to you. If the order has been suspended and the defendant still does not pay, use form N446 to request re-issue of the process so that the court will send the order to his employer. No fee is charged for this.

You cannot obtain an attachment of earnings order against a defendant who is in the army, navy or air force or is a merchant seaman, a firm or a limited company. Nor can you obtain one against a defendant who is self-employed or unemployed. If the defendant is on a very low wage it might not be possible for the court to make such an order.

If the defendant has found new work after a period of unemployment during which the order had lapsed you can use form N446 to ask the court to send the attachment of earnings order to the new employer.

A Garnishee Order

If you have obtained a judgement for more than £25 the court can order a person who owes the defendant money or who holds money on their behalf to pay you as much as is needed to cover the balance on your judgement, or if there is not sufficient to pay you as much as they have or owe.

A garnishee order can apply to most debts but is normally used to obtain money from a defendant's bank or building society accounts. You should fill in form N349 giving the name and address of the person who owes the defendant money or the name and branch of the defendant's bank if you know it. The form must then be sworn on oath. This can be done before a court officer at any county court free of charge or before a solicitor who will charge you a small fee.

There will not be a hearing. A district judge will consider your application. If he decides to grant the order the court will send a garnishee order nisi to the person who owes or holds the money for the defendant. This person is known as the garnishee. This order will freeze the account. You will be sent a copy and the defendant will also be sent one seven days later.

Before the money is paid to the claimant the defendant and the garnishee will have the opportunity to tell the court if there are any good reasons why the garnishee order nisi should not be made absolute. For example the money really belongs to someone else or the account is overdrawn. If they do not have a reason the court will make a garnishee order absolute which will mean the garnishee has to pay the money to the claimant.

The order only freezes the money that was credited to the defendant on the date when the bank or person received the order. It does not cover money paid in later. Therefore it is a good idea to try and have it served when they are likely to have as much money as possible for example at the beginning of the month if that is when their salary is paid.

A Charging Order & Order for Sale

If the defendant does not have identifiable income or money for you to claim but does own property such as a house (either freehold or leasehold) or something such as bonds, stocks and shares, you can obtain a charging order over this property. The effect would be that you would have a right to part of the value of the property and when it is sold you will receive your money.

To obtain a charging order you must prove that the debtor owns the property. In the case of land this means obtaining "Office Copy Entries" from HM Land Registry for which you will need to complete a "Public Index Map" search to find out the title number of the land. This order provides security for the debt and is equivalent to a mortgage. The order must be registered at HMLR to be effective against land.

Unlike the other types of enforcement proceedings there is no application form for a charging order. You should therefore use the general application form N244 supported by evidence i.e. a witness statement saying that the defendant owes you money and giving the details of the court order. The court fee is £50

You should also say that the debt is a result of a judgement and give the date, case number and details of the judgement. State what the outstanding balance of the debt is, then send the affidavit to the court with the document from the and registry and the fee.

Once you have a charging order you can ask the court to order the defendant to sell his property to pay the debt. This is a separate procedure under CPR Part 8 using form N288. You will therefore issue separate proceedings for a fixed date hearing (i.e. default judgement is not available) and pay another fee. In practice it is difficult to obtain such an order. The court is unlikely to order the sale of a valuable property or family home to pay a small debt. You are likely to find that the defendant's home is jointly owned with his or her spouse. Even if they are not registered as a legal owner a husband or wife can have rights over a house known as a "beneficial interest" which could stop you obtaining an order for sale. Furthermore the property is likely to be mortgaged and the mortgagee may well oppose the sale. You should take advice before applying for a charging order and especially before applying for an order for sale because these procedures can be complicated and costly.

Oral Examination

This is not a method of enforcement but is a means of finding out information about the defendant to enable you to decide if he is able to pay you and which method of enforcement would be most appropriate. You can request an oral examination by filling in form N316 and sending it to the defendant's local court with the fee. If you obtained your judgement in a different court you must first write to that original court asking for the case to be transferred, and then send your form and fee in once this has been done.

If the defendant is a company you can request an oral examination of one of the directors. You can find out who the directors are by telephoning Companies House on 029 20380801. The case should be transferred to the court nearest the director's home or business address rather than the one nearest to the company's registered office.

The court will send the defendant a form telling him when to attend court and instructing him to bring any documents concerning his finances. The court may also send out a questionnaire for the defendant to complete prior to the hearing.

You will be notified of when the examination is to take place. Check whether you are required to attend. If you cannot but you have specific questions that you would like the defendant to be asked write to the court and ask that they be included in the examination. You will receive a copy of the defendant's answers after the examination.

If the defendant fails to attend the examination will normally be adjourned and rescheduled for a new date. If this happens you may have to pay the defendant's reasonable travelling expenses to attend on the new date, known as "conduct money". The defendant is entitled to ask you for this at any time up to seven days before the date fixed for the adjourned examination.

It is important that you write to the court just prior to the examination (no more than four days beforehand) to let them know that you have paid a reasonable amount for travelling expenses or that the defendant has not asked you for conduct money. If you have paid his expenses and the defendant fails to attend that amount will be added to what he owes you.

An order to attend an adjourned oral examination must be served personally by a bailiff. If the defendant fails to attend the judge can issue a warrant for his rrest provided that he is satisfied the defendant knew of the examination. The bailiff will then arrest the defendant and bring him to the court to be examined. The court will send you a copy of his answers.

Appointment of a Receiver

Receivership orders are made where it is not impossible to use any of the other legal methods of enforcement. The order will authorise the receiver to receive money, rent and profits which the judgement debtor is entitled to because of his interest in specified property. When deciding whether or not to appoint a receiver the court will take into account the amount that is owed, the amount that is likely to be obtained by a receiver and the probable costs of the appointment. It is not a usual course of action for recovering debts arising out of small claims.

Bankruptcy Proceedings

Non payment of the debt could give you grounds to issue a bankruptcy petition against the defendant. The debt must exceed £750, it must be unsecured and the debtor must either be unable to pay or have no reasonable prospect of being able to pay.

Claimant's Obligations

If you have begun any of the enforcement proceedings and you receive full or partial payment from the defendant you must tell the court immediately.

14

IF JUDGMENT HAS BEEN
ENTERED AGAINST YOU

---

f you were unsuccessful in your case and an order has been made that you should pay your opponent you should send the payments directly to him or his representative. The name and address for payment will be shown on the court forms. You should not send payments to the court. The judgement order will tell you when to pay and if it should be by instalments. It is important that you pay on time because if you are late, even by one day, the claimant will be able to ask the court to take the steps outlined in the previous chapter and you are likely to have to pay the costs of such action.

Always allow plenty of time for the payment to arrive. The courts recommend you allow at least four clear working days before it is due. You should pay by cheque or postal order or some other method which gives you proof you have paid. Do not send cash. You should keep a record of all the payments you make and when you send them enclose your name, address, case number and claimant's reference with your payment.

Varying the Order

f you have been ordered to pay the whole judgement debt as one lump sum or by instalments that are too large you can use form N244 to ask the court to vary the order and reduce the payments. The claimant will be asked if he will agree to accept what you are offering to pay. If he will not the court will decide what you should pay. If you do not accept their decision you should write within sixteen days of the date of the postmark on the varied order giving your reasons and asking that the matter should be reconsidered. A hearing with a district judge will be arranged at your local court where the matter will be decided.

Inability to Pay

If you have no income and cannot pay anything towards the debt at the moment ask the court for a stay of judgement on form N244. A hearing with a district judge will be arranged.

Suspension of Warrants & Orders

When the claimant tries to recover money using one of the enforcement procedures outlined in the previous chapter you will have the opportunity to apply for the warrant or order to be suspended.

The Register of County Court Judgements

The judgement will be entered on the County Court Judgements Register and will remain there for six years. This may make it difficult for you to obtain credit, a mortgage or goods on hire purchase. Banks, building societies and credit companies search the Register. The Office of Fair Trading produces a booklet called "No Credit" explaining what you can do if you are refused credit. You can telephone them on 020 8398 3405 to ask for a copy.

If you pay the full amount you owe within one month of the judgement date, you can ask the court to take your name off the register. You will have to pay a

e of £3 and give the court proof that you have paid, for example a letter from
e claimant. The court will cancel your entry on the register and give you a
ertificate of satisfaction to prove that you paid within one month. If you do not
ay within one month you can ask the court to mark the register "satisfied"
hen you have paid the full amount that you owe. This will mean that anyone
ho searches the register will know you have paid the debt and when your last
ayment was made. You will receive a certificate of satisfaction but the entry
ill remain on the register for six years. To obtain this send the fee of £3 and
roof of payment.

Administration Orders

you have at least two outstanding debts and at least one of them is a result of
judgement you can apply to the court for an administration order using form
92. To be eligible the total sum of your debts must not be more than £5,000.
he effect of a small claims track order would be that the court would help you
administer your finances and in the meantime none of your creditors would
able to take enforcement action or to make you bankrupt without referring to
e court first.

an administration order is made instead of paying for creditors directly you
ould make monthly payments to the court which would then divide the
oney between your creditors. The court will decide how much you have to
ay after considering the information you give about your income and
xpenditure in your application form.

ou can suggest a rate at which you could pay but be realistic. Make sure it is
amount you really can afford and that you have allowed yourself enough for
our basic needs.

If you have a job the court might make an order that your employer shoul deduct money from your earnings and send it straight to them. If you do nc want this to happen indicate on your application form that you do not want a attachment of earnings order.

Fill in the form but do not sign it then take it to your local county court wher you will be asked to swear on oath that the information you have given in you application is true and to sign the form in front of a court officer. If you hav any documents which support your statements about your income an expenditure take them with you, for example bills and receipts.

When the court has fixed a rate of payment you and your creditors will b given 16 days in which to object. If anyone does object a hearing will b arranged.

If you have trouble paying the amount ordered contact the court immediately If you fail to pay the court has the power to issue a warrant of execution, t make an attachment of earnings order or to revoke the administration order i which case your creditors can enforce their rights themselves. If you incu more debts after the order has been made these can only be added with th agreement of the court.

The administration order will be entered on the register of county cou judgements that will mean you are likely to find it difficult to obtain credit unt your debts are paid.

A Composition Order

When an administration order has been made the court may, in som circumstances, make an order that you do not have to pay the full amour which you owe. It reduces proportionately the amount owed to your various creditors.

Individual Voluntary Arrangements

You can suggest a Voluntary Arrangement which is a legally binding contract between you and your unsecured creditors. You can make a proposal for payment but it only becomes binding once the creditors have accepted it. The creditors do not have to receive the full amount due but it must be more than they would receive under your bankruptcy.

You can ask for an interim order to stay all proceedings while the creditors consider the proposal but you will need an insolvency practitioner to make the application for you which will be expensive.

Bankruptcy

An individual can file his own petition to make himself bankrupt on a voluntary basis. There is a fee of £275 for this and you will need to produce a statement of affairs disclosing all assets and liabilities, and fill in a form for the court. When a debtor owes under £20,000 and is made bankrupt voluntarily rather than at the request of his creditors he may be an undischarged bankrupt for only two years rather than the usual three. Bankruptcy has serious consequences and you would be ill advised to make such an application without seeking advice.

15

THE COSTS OF THE SMALL CLAIMS TRACK

County Court Fees

These are fees that must be paid to the court to commence and enforce your claim. When you issue a claim form and you are only claiming money the amount of the fee is determined by the size of your claim, as outlined below:

Claim		Fee
Up to	£200	£27
	£300	£38
	£400	£50
	£500	£60
	£1,000	£80
	£5,000	£115

To issue proceedings where you are claiming something other than money, such as an injunction the fee is £65. You can include a claim for money without paying an additional fee. These fees are current as at 2000 but it may be necessary to check with your local courts for details of fees.

Counterclaims

If you are making a counterclaim you will have to pay a fee if the amount you are claiming is more than the sum being claimed from you. To calculate the amount you should work out the ordinary fee for a claim of that size and then deduct the fees paid by the claimant. You will have to pay the difference. For example if the counterclaim is £500 the ordinary fee for a claim of that size would be £50. However, if the claimant's claim is for £400, it will have been subject to a fee of £40. The defendant must pay the difference of £10. The same method of calculation is used to work out the fees payable for the enforcement of counterclaims.

Service by a Court Bailiff

Having documents served by a court bailiff carries a fee of £10 for each person served. This applies even if a number of people are served at the same address.

Setting Aside Awards

If you make an application to set aside an award made by an district judge a fee of £20 will be payable.

Enforcing Judgements

If you have succeeded in obtaining a judgement against someone and they have not complied with the courts order you may issue enforcement proceedings to make them fulfil their obligations. The fees are:

- A warrant to recover a sum not more than £125   £20

- A warrant to recover a sum over £125   £40

- A warrant for the recovery of property (a possession)   £80

- To issue an application for an attachment of earnings order £50

- To issue an application for a charging order £50

- To issue an application for a garnishee order £25

- To issue a judgement claim form £25

- To issue an application for an oral examination £30

You do not have to pay court fees if you are receiving income support at the time the fee is paid. This exemption applies even if you are receiving legal advice and assistance under the "Green form Scheme" but not if you are in receipt of legal representation under Part IV of the Legal Aid Act 1988 for the purpose of proceedings.

You may also be exempt from paying fees, at the discretion of the Chief Clerk, if you can show that paying the fee would cause undue hardship because of the exceptional circumstances of the case.

Recovering Costs From Your Opponent

Small claims are an exception to the usual practice where in general if you win your case your opponent pays you costs. In small claims even if you are entirely successful only a few of your possible expenses will be recoverable. They are:

- The costs which were stated on the claim form or which would have been on the claim form if the claim had been for a liquidated sum.

- Up to £200 in respect of the fees of an expert. Inclusive of VAT.

- Up to £260 for legal advice obtained to bring or defend a claim for an injunction, specific performance or similar relief. Inclusive of VAT.

- Up to £50 in respect of a party's or a witness's loss of earnings when attending a hearing.

- Any expenses which have been reasonably incurred by a party or a witness in travelling to and from the hearing or in staying away from home.

- The costs of enforcing the award.

- Such further costs as a district judge may direct where there has been unreasonable conduct on the part of the opposite party in relation to the proceedings or a claim that was made. An example of unreasonable conduct would be the fabrication of a wholly untruthful defence.

Injunctions & Specific Performance

The provision of the county court rule which governs automatic reference to small claims track refers to actions where there is a "sum claimed" or "amount involved", thus it is arguable that if you are not claiming money but only seeking an injunction or specific performance your case should not be automatically referred to small claims track. If the case is not dealt with as a small claim this could mean it would be easier for you to claim legal aid, and more importantly that if you win your case you could recover your costs from your opponent. Consequently if you are claiming a small amount in damages with your injunction it may actually save you money to forego the damages claim. Such considerations can be complex and difficult and you would put yourself at risk of paying your opponents costs if you lose so take advice from a solicitor on this question. Remember £260 spent in advance is recoverable even if the case proceeds as a small claim.

Housing Matters

If you have a housing dispute for example, for nuisance or disrepair, you may be able to bring a claim in the magistrates court under the Environmental Protection Act 1990 as an alternative to small claims track. You can claim up to £5,000 in damages and get a nuisance order, which is equivalent to specific performance. Legal aid is not available but if you are successful you can claim your legal costs from your opponent.

GLOSSARY

Action	The name given to legal proceedings
Allocation Questionnaire	The form received issued by the court when a defence is filed
Attachment of Earnings	Enforcement of a judgement debt by deducting payments from salary or earnings
Bailiff	The court officer who enforces court orders and serves court documents
Burden of Proof	The term which means that the claimant must prove his case. A defendant must prove the case by counter-claim
Case reference	The number given to each case quoted on all correspondence

Charging Order	Enforcement of a judgement by a mortgage
Chief Clerk	The administrator of the court to whom all letters should be addressed
Claimant	The party who starts an action
Counterclaim	A separate claim made by the defendant against the claimant
County Court	The civil court which conducts small claims tracks of small claims
Damages	The legal term for the compensation that the court orders the successful party to pay the unsuccessful party
Defendant	The party who is sued
Defence	The rejection of a claim filed by the defendant

Directions	Court-orders informing the parties of any preliminary action to take before the small claims track
District judge	The judge who will act as arbiter at the small claims track of the small claim
Evidence	The process by which the facts of a case are established, for the benefit of the judge. Evidence may be oral or documentary
Expert	A person who has an expertise which is recognised by the court
Expert evidence	Evidence given by an expert to support a case, consisting of an expert report and oral evidence

Form of Admission	The court form used by the defendant to admit or partially admit a claim, and to offer payment by instalments
Form of Defence &	The form used by the defendant to Counter-claim file a defence or counter-claim
Garnishee Order	An enforcement order requiring a creditor of the judgement debtor to pay monies into court on account of the debt to the successful party
Judgement	The appropriate court's determination of a case ordering the parties to take certain action, usually a payment of money
Party or parties	Claimant or defendant

Onus of Proof	The obligation to answer or rebut allegations made by the other side
Open letter	A letter offering a settlement which is intended to be binding, compared to a "without prejudice" letter or offer
Oral Examination	An examination of a debtor on oath in court whereby a successful party asks questions with a view to choosing suitable methods or remedies of enforcement
Order for Sale	An order enforcing a charging order and is rare
Pre-Trial Review	A pre-hearing ordered by the district judge, unusual in small claims

Prove	To give evidence which "on the balance of all probabilities" shows that an argument is correct.
Request for Judgement	The form filed by the in Default claimant when the claim form is ignored
Service	Delivering the court documents to the other side
Small Claim	A monetary claim of less than £5,000
Warrant of Execution	Enforcement whereby the court bailiff seizes goods belonging to the debtor for sale
Without prejudice	An offer which is not binding

APPENDIX 1

Practice Directions 1998

PRACTICE DIRECTION – HOW TO START PROCEEDINGS – THE CLAIM FORM

THIS PRACTICE DIRECTION SUPPLEMENTS CPR PART 7

GENERAL

1   Omitted

WHERE TO START PROCEEDINGS

2.1 to 2.10 Omitted

THE CLAIM FORM

3.1   A claimant must use practice form N1 or practice form N208 (the Part 8 claim form) to start a claim (but see paragraphs 3.2 and 3.4 below).

3.2   to 3.7 Omitted

3.8   If a claim for damages for personal injuries is started in the county court, the claim form must state whether or not the claimant expects to recover more than £1000 in respect of pain, suffering and loss of amenity.

3.9   If a claim for housing disrepair which includes a claim for an order requiring repairs or other work to be carried out by the landlord is started in the county court, the claim form must state:

(1)   whether or not the cost of the repairs or other work is estimated to be more than £1000, and

(2)   whether or not the claimant expects to recover more than £1000 in respect of any claim for damages[2].

If either of the amounts mentioned in (1) and (2) is more than £1000, the small claims track will not be the normal track for that claim.

TITLE OF PROCEEDINGS

4.1   and 4.2 Omitted

START OF PROCEEDINGS

5.1   to 5.5 Omitted

PARTICULARS OF CLAIM

6.1   Where the claimant does not include the particulars of claim in the claim form, particulars of claim may be served separately:

(1)   either at the same time as the claim form, or

(2)   within 14 days after service of the claim form provided that the service of the particulars of claim is within 4 months after the date of issue of the claim form[5] (or 6 months where the claim form is to be served out of the jurisdiction[6]).

6.2   If the particulars of claim are not included in or have not been served with the claim form, the claim form must contain a statement that particulars of claim will follow[7].

STATEMENT OF TRUTH

7.1   Part 22 requires the claim form and, where they are not included in the claim form, the particulars of claim, to be verified by a statement of truth.

7.2 The form of the statement of truth is as follows: '[I believe][the claimant believes] that the facts stated in [this claim form] [these particulars of claim] are true.'

7.3 Attention is drawn to rule 32.14 which sets out the consequences of verifying a statement of case containing a false statement without an honest belief in its truth.

EXTENSION OF TIME

8.1 and 8.2 Omitted

PRACTICE DIRECTION – CONSUMER CREDIT ACT CLAIM

THIS PRACTICE DIRECTION SUPPLEMENTS CPR RULE 7.9

1.1 to 7.2 Omitted

7.3 A claimant who is a debtor or hirer making a claim for an order under section 129(1)(b) of the Act (a time order) must state (in the following order) in his particulars of claim:

(1) the date of the agreement,

(2) the parties to the agreement,

(3) the number or other means of identifying the agreement,

(4) details of any sureties,

(5) if the defendant is not one of the original parties to the agreement then the name of the original party to the agreement,

(6) the names and addresses of the persons intended to be served with the claim form,

(7) the place where the claimant signed the agreement,

(8)   details of the notice served by the creditor or owner giving rise to the claim for the time order,

(9)   the total unpaid balance the claimant admits is due under the agreement, and –

  (a)   the amount of any arrears (if known), and

  (b)   the amount and frequency of the payments specified in the agreement, (10) the claimant's proposals for payments of any arrears and of future installments together with details of his means;

(11)   where the claim relates to a breach of the agreement other than for the payment of money the claimant's proposals for remedying it.

7.4   Omitted

ADMISSION OF CERTAIN CLAIMS FOR RECOVERY OF GOODS UNDER REGULATED AGREEMENTS

8.1   to 8.7 Omitted

ADDITIONAL REQUIREMENTS ABOUT PARTIES TO THE PROCEEDINGS

9.1   to 9.5 Omitted

NOTICE TO BE GIVEN TO RE-OPEN A CONSUMER CREDIT AGREEMENT

10.1 Where a debtor or any surety intends to apply for a consumer credit agreement to be reopened after a claim on or relating to the agreement has already begun, and:

(1)   section 139(1)(b)4 ; or

(2)   section 139(1)(c),

applies, the debtor or surety must serve written notice of his intention on the court and every other party to the proceedings within 14 days of the service of the claim form on him.

10.2 If the debtor or surety (as the case may be) serves a notice under paragraph

10.1 he will be treated as having filed a defence for the purposes of the Consumer Credit Act procedure.

PRACTICE DIRECTION – ACKNOWLEDGMENT OF SERVICE

THIS PRACTICE DIRECTION SUPPLEMENTS CPR PART 10

RESPONDING TO THE CLAIM

1.1 Part 9 sets out how a defendant may respond to a claim.

1.2 Part 10 sets out the provisions for acknowledging service (but see rule 8.3 for information about acknowledging service of a claim under the Part 8 procedure).

THE FORM OF ACKNOWLEDGMENT OF SERVICE

2 A defendant who wishes to acknowledge service of a claim should do so by using form N9.

ADDRESS FOR SERVICE

3.1 The defendant must include in his acknowledgment of service an address for the service of documents [1].

3.2 Where the defendant is represented by a legal representative [2] and the legal representative has signed the acknowledgment of service form, the address must be the legal representative's business address

SIGNING THE ACKNOWLEDGMENT OF SERVICE

4.1 An acknowledgment of service must be signed by the defendant or by his legal representative.

4.2 Where the defendant is a company or other corporation, a person holding a senior position in the company or corporation may sign the acknowledgment of service on the defendant's behalf, but must state the position he holds.

4.3 to 4.5 Omitted

GENERAL

5.1 The defendant's name should be set out in full on the acknowledgment of service.

5.2 Where the defendant's name has been incorrectly set out in the claim form, it should be correctly set out on the acknowledgment of service followed by the words 'described as' and the incorrect name.

5.3 If two or more defendants to a claim acknowledge service of a claim through the same legal representative at the same time, only one acknowledgment of service need be used.

5.4 An acknowledgment of service may be amended or withdrawn only with the permission of the court.

5.5 Omitted

PRACTICE DIRECTION – DEFAULT JUDGMENT

THIS PRACTICE DIRECTION SUPPLEMENTS CPR PART 12

DEFAULT JUDGMENT

1.1 A default judgment is judgment without a trial where a defendant has failed to file either:

(1) an acknowledgment of service, or

(2) a defence.

For this purpose a defence includes any document purporting to be a defence.

1.2 & 1.3 Omitted

OBTAINING DEFAULT JUDGMENT

2.1 to 2.3 Omitted.

DEFAULT JUDGMENT BY REQUEST

3 Omitted

EVIDENCE

4.1 Both on a request and on an application for default judgment the court must be satisfied that:

(1) the particulars of claim have been served on the defendant (a certificate of service on the court file will be sufficient evidence),

(2) either the defendant has not filed an acknowledgment of service or has not filed a defence and that in either case the relevant period for doing so has expired,

(3) the defendant has not satisfied the claim, and

(4) the defendant has not returned an admission to the claimant under rule or filed an admission with the court under rule 14.6.

4.2 to 4.6 Omitted

PRACTICE DIRECTION – ADMISSIONS

THIS PRACTICE DIRECTION SUPPLEMENTS CPR PART 14

ADMISSIONS GENERALLY

1.1 and 1.2 Omitted

FORMS

2.1 & 2.2 Omitted

RETURNING OR FILING THE ADMISSION

3.1 If the defendant wishes to make an admission in respect of the whole of a claim for a specified amount of money, the admission form or other written notice of the admission should be completed and returned to the claimant within 14 days of service of the particulars of claim [2].

3.2 If the defendant wishes to make an admission in respect of a part of a claim for a specified amount of money, or in respect of a claim for an unspecified amount of money, the admission form or other written notice of admission should be completed and filed with the court within 14 days of service of the particulars of claim [3].

3.3 The defendant may also file a defence under rule 15.2.

REQUEST FOR TIME TO PAY

4.1　A defendant who makes an admission in respect of a claim for a specified sum of money or offers to pay a sum of money in respect of a claim for an unspecified sum may, in the admission form, make a request for time to pay[4].

4.2　If the claimant accepts the defendant's request he may obtain judgment by filing a request for judgment contained in Form N225A[5]; the court will then enter judgment for payment at the time and rate specified in the defendant's request[6].

4.3　If the claimant does not accept the request for time to pay, he should file notice to that effect by completing Form N225A; the court will then enter judgment for the amount of the admission (less any payments made) at a time and rate of payment decided by the court (see rule 14.10).

DETERMINING THE RATE OF PAYMENT

5.1　In deciding the time and rate of payment the court will take into account:

(1)　the defendant's statement of means set out in the admission form or in any other written notice of the admission filed,

(2)　the claimant's objections to the defendant's request set out in the claimant's notice[7], and

(3)　any other relevant factors.

5.2　The time and rate of payment may be decided:

(1)　by a judge with or without a hearing, or

(2)　by a court officer without a hearing provided that –

(a)　the only claim is for a specified sum of money, and

(b) the amount outstanding is not more than £50,000 (including costs).

5.3 Where a decision has been made without a hearing whether by a court officer or by a judge, either party may apply for the decision to be re-determined by a judge [8].

5.4 If the decision was made by a court officer the re-determination may take place without a hearing, unless a hearing is requested in the application notice.

5.5 If the decision was made by a judge the re-determination must be made at a hearing unless the parties otherwise agree.

5.6 Rule 14.13(2) describes how to apply for a re-determination.

VARYING THE RATE OF PAYMENT

6.1 Either party may, on account of a change in circumstances since the date of the decision (or re-determination as the case may be) apply to vary the time and rate of payment of installments still remaining unpaid.

6.2 An application to vary under paragraph 6.1 above should be made in accordance with Part 23.

PRACTICE DIRECTION – DEFENCE AND REPLY

THIS PRACTICE DIRECTION SUPPLEMENTS CPR PART 15

DEFENDING THE CLAIM

1.1 & 2.2 Omitted

1.3 Form N9B (specified amount) or N9D (unspecified amount or non-money claims) may be used for the purpose of defence and is included in the response pack served on the defendant with the particulars of claim.

1.4   Attention is drawn to rule 15.3 which sets out a possible consequence of not filing a defence.

STATEMENT OF TRUTH

2.1   Part 22 requires a defence to be verified by a statement of truth.

2.2   The form of the statement of truth is as follows: '[I believe][the defendant believes] that the facts stated in this defence are true.'

2.3   Attention is drawn to rule 32.14 which sets out the consequences of verifying a statement of case containing a false statement without an honest belief in its truth.

GENERAL

3.1   Where a defendant to a claim serves a counterclaim under Part 20, the defence and counterclaim should normally form one document with the counterclaim following on from the defence.

3.2   Where a claimant serves a reply and a defence to counterclaim, the reply and defence to counterclaim should normally form one document with the defence to counterclaim following on from the reply.

3.2A   Rule 15.8(a) provides that a claimant must file any reply with his allocation questionnaire. Where the date by which he must file his allocation questionnaire is later than the date by which he must file his defence to counterclaim (because the time for filing the allocation questionnaire under rule 26.3(6) is more than 14 days after the date on which it is deemed to be served), the court will normally order that the defence to counterclaim must be filed by the same date as the reply. Where the court does not make such an order the reply and defence to counterclaim may form separate documents.

3.3 & 3.4 Omitted

PRACTICE DIRECTION – STATEMENTS OF CASE

THIS PRACTICE DIRECTION SUPPLEMENTS CPR PART 16

GENERAL

1.1 & 1.2 omitted

THE CLAIM FORM

2.1 Rule 16.2 refers to matters which the claim form must contain. Where the claim is for money, the claim form must also contain the statement of value referred to in rule 16.3.

2.2 Where the defendant is an individual, the claimant should (if he is able to do so) include in the claim form an address at which the defendant resides or carries on business. This paragraph applies even though the defendant's solicitors have agreed to accept service on the defendant's behalf.

PARTICULARS OF CLAIM

3.1 If practicable, the particulars of claim should be set out in the claim form.

3.2 Where the claimant does not include the particulars of claim in the claim form, particulars of claim may be served separately:

(1) either at the same time as the claim form, or

(2) within 14 days after service of the claim form[1] provided that the service of the particulars of claim is not later than 4

months from the date of issue of the claim form[2] (or 6 months where the claim form is to be served out of the jurisdiction[3]).

3.3 If the particulars of claim are not included in or have not been served with the claim form, the claim form must also contain a statement that particulars of claim will follow[4].

3.4 Particulars of claim which are not included in the claim form must be verified by a statement of truth, the form of which is as follows: '[I believe][the claimant believes] that the facts stated in these particulars of claim are true.'

3.5 Attention is drawn to rule 32.14 which sets out the consequences of verifying a statement of case containing a false statement without an honest belief in its truth.

3.6 The full particulars of claim must include:

(1) the matters set out in rule 16.4, and

(2) where appropriate, the matters set out in practice directions relating to specific types of claims.

3.7 Attention is drawn to the provisions of rule 16.4(2) in respect of a claim for interest.

3.8 Particulars of claim served separately from the claim form must also contain:

(1) the name of the court in which the claim is proceeding,

(2) the claim number,

(3) the title of the proceedings, and

(4) the claimant's address for service.

MATTERS WHICH MUST BE INCLUDED IN THE PARTICULARS OF CLAIM IN CERTAIN TYPES OF CLAIM

Personal injury claims

4.1 The particulars of claim must contain:

   (1) the claimant's date of birth, and

   (2) brief details of the claimant's personal injuries.

4.2 The claimant must attach to his particulars of claim a schedule of details of any past and future expenses and losses which he claims.

4.3 Where the claimant is relying on the evidence of a medical practitioner the claimant must attach to or serve with his particulars of claim a report from a medical practitioner about the personal injuries which he alleges in his claim.

4.4 Omitted

Fatal accident claims

5.1 to 5.3 Omitted

Recovery of land

6 Omitted

Hire purchase claims

7.1 & 7.2 Omitted

OTHER MATTERS TO BE INCLUDED IN PARTICULARS OF CLAIM

8.1 & 8.2 Omitted

8.3 Where a claim is based upon a written agreement:

   (1) a copy of the contract or documents constituting the agreement should be

attached to or served with the particulars of claim and the original(s) should be available at the hearing, and

(2) any general conditions of sale incorporated in the contract should also be attached (but where the contract is or the documents constituting the agreement are bulky this practice direction is complied with by attaching or serving only the relevant parts of the contract or documents).

8.4 Where a claim is based upon an oral agreement, the particulars of claim should set out the contractual words used and state by whom, to whom, when and where they were spoken.

8.5 Where a claim is based upon an agreement by conduct, the particulars of claim must specify the conduct relied on and state by whom, when and where the acts constituting the conduct were done.

8.6 In a claim issued in the High Court relating to a Consumer Credit Agreement, the particulars of claim must contain a statement that the action is not one to which section 141 of the Consumer Credit Act 1974 applies.

MATTERS WHICH MUST BE SPECIFICALLY SET OUT IN THE PARTICULARS OF CLAIM IF RELIED ON

9.1 & 9.2 Omitted

GENERAL

10.1 Omitted

10.2 A subsequent statement of case must not contradict or be inconsistent with an earlier one; for example a reply to a defence must not bring in a new claim. Where new matters have come to light the appropriate course may be to seek the court's permission to amend the statement of case.

THE DEFENCE

General

11.1 Rule 16.5 deals with the contents of the defence.

11.2 A defendant should deal with every allegation in accordance with rule 16.5(1) and (2).

11.3 Rule 16.5(3), (4) and (5) sets out the consequences of not dealing with an allegation.

11.4 Where the defendant is an individual, and the claim form does not contain an address at which he resides or carries on business, or contains an incorrect address, the defendant must provide such an address in the defence.

11.5 Where the defendant's address for service is not where he resides or carries on business, he must still provide the address required by paragraph 11.4.

Statement of truth

12.1 Part 22 requires a defence to be verified by a statement of truth.

12.2 The form of the statement of truth is as follows: '[I believe][the defendant believes] that the facts stated in the defence are true.'

12.3 Attention is drawn to rule 32.14 which sets out the consequences of verifying a statement of case containing a false statement without an honest belief in its truth.

MATTERS WHICH MUST BE INCLUDED IN THE DEFENCE

Personal injury claims

13.1 Where the claim is for personal injuries and the claimant has attached a medical report in respect of his alleged injuries, the defendant should:

(1) state in his defence whether he –

(a) agrees,

(b) disputes, or

(c) neither agrees nor disputes but has no knowledge of,

the matters contained in the medical report,

(2) where he disputes any part of the medical report, give in his defence his reasons for doing so, and

(3) where he has obtained his own medical report on which he intends to rely, attach it to his defence.

13.2 Where the claim is for personal injuries and the claimant has included a schedule of past and future expenses and losses, the defendant should include in or attach to his defence a counter-schedule stating:

(1) which of those items he –

(a) agrees,

(b) disputes, or

(c) neither agrees nor disputes but has no knowledge of, and

(2) where any items are disputed, supplying alternative figures where appropriate.

14.1   The defendant must give details of the expiry of any relevant limitation period relied on.

14.2   Rule 37.3 and paragraph 2 of the practice direction which supplements Part 37 contains information about a defence of tender.

14.3   A party may:

(1)   refer in his statement of case to any point of law on which his claim or defence, as the case may be, is based,

(2)   give in his statement of case the name of any witness he proposes to call, and

(3)   attach to or serve with this statement of case a copy of any document which he considers is necessary to his claim or defence, as the case may be (including any expert's report to be filed in accordance with Part 35).

OMPETITION ACT 1998

15   Omitted

RACTICE DIRECTION – COUNTERCLAIMS AND OTHER PART 20 CLAIMS

THIS PRACTICE DIRECTION SUPPLEMENTS CPR PART 20

A Part 20 claim is any claim other than the claim by the claimant against the defendant.

ASES WHERE COURT'S PERMISSION TO MAKE A PART 20 CLAIM IS EQUIRED

1.1   Rules 20.4(2)(b), 20.5(1) and 20.7(3)(b) set out the circumstances in which the court's permission will be needed for making a Part 20 claim.

1.2 Where an application is made for permission to make a Part 20 claim the application notice should be filed together with a copy of the proposed Part 20 claim.

APPLICATIONS FOR PERMISSION TO ISSUE A PART 20 CLAIM

2.1 An application for permission to make a Part 20 claim must be supported by evidence stating:

(1) the stage which the action has reached,

(2) the nature of the claim to be made by the Part 20 claimant or details of the question or issue which needs to be decided,

(3) a summary of the facts on which the Part 20 claim is based, and

(4) the name and address of the proposed Part 20 defendant.

2.2 Where delay has been a factor contributing to the need to apply for permission to make a Part 20 claim an explanation of the delay should be given in evidence.

2.3 Where possible the applicant should provide a timetable of the action to date.

2.4 Rules 20.5(2) and 20.7(5) allow applications to be made to the court without notice unless the court otherwise directs.

GENERAL

3 The Civil Procedure Rules apply generally to Part 20 claims as if they were claims 1 . Parties should be aware that the provisions relating to failure to respond will apply.

STATEMENT OF TRUTH

4.1 The contents of a Part 20 claim should be verified by a statement of truth. Part 22 requires a statement of case to be verified by a statement of truth.

4.2 The form of the statement of truth should be as follows: '[I believe][the [Part 20 claimant]* believes] that the facts stated in this statement of case are true, *(For the purpose of this practice direction the Part 20 claimant means any party making a Part 20 claim.)

4.3 Attention is drawn to rule 32.14 which sets out the consequences of verifying a statement of case containing a false statement without an honest belief in its truth.

(For information regarding statements of truth see Part 22 and the practice direction which supplements it.)

CASE MANAGEMENT WHERE THERE IS A PART 20 DEFENCE

5.1 to 5.4 Omitted

FORM OF COUNTERCLAIM

6.1 Where a defendant to a claim serves a counterclaim under this Part, the defence and counterclaim should normally form one document with the counterclaim following on from the defence.

6.2 Where a claimant serves a reply and a defence to counterclaim, the reply and the defence to counterclaim should normally form one document with the defence to counterclaim following on from the reply.

TITLES OF PROCEEDINGS WHERE THERE ARE PART 20 CLAIMS

7.1 to 7.6 Omitted

PRACTICE DIRECTION – SMALL CLAIMS TRACK

THIS PRACTICE DIRECTION SUPPLEMENTS CPR PART 27

JUDGES

1   The functions of the court described in Part 2 which are to be carried out by a judge w generally be carried out by a district judge b may be carried out by a Circuit Judge.

CASE MANAGEMENT DIRECTIONS

2.1   Rule 27.4 explains how directions will be give and rule 27.6 contains provisions about th holding of a preliminary hearing and the cour powers at such a hearing.

2.2   Appendix A sets out the Standard Direction which the court may give.

REPRESENTATION AT A HEARING

3.1   In this paragraph:

(1)   a lawyer means a barrister, a solicitor or legal executive employed by a solicitc and

(2)   a lay representative means any oth person.

3.2   (1)   A party may present his own case at hearing or a lawyer or lay representativ may present it for him.

(2)   The Lay Representatives (Right Audience) Order 1999 provides that a la representative may not exercise any rig of audience:–

(a) where his client does not attend the hearing;

(b) at any stage after judgment; or

(c) on any appeal brought against any decision made by the district judge in the proceedings.

(3) However the court, exercising its general discretion to hear anybody, may hear a lay representative even in circumstances excluded by the Order.

(4) Any of its officers or employees may represent a corporate party.

SMALL CLAIM HEARING

4.1 (1) The general rule is that a small claim hearing will be in public.

(2) The judge may decide to hold it in private if:

(a) the parties agree, or

(b) a ground mentioned in rule 39.2(3) applies.

(3) A hearing or part of a hearing which takes place other than at the court, for example at the home or business premises of a party, will not be in public.

4.2 A hearing that takes place at the court will generally be in the judge's room but it may take place in a courtroom.

4.3 Rule 27.8 allows the court to adopt any method of proceeding that it considers to be fair and to limit cross-examination. The judge may in particular:

(1) ask questions of any witness himself before allowing any other person to do so,

(2) ask questions of all or any of the witnesses himself before allowing any other person to ask questions of any witnesses,

(3) refuse to allow cross-examination of any witness until all the witnesses have given evidence in chief,

(4) limit cross-examination of a witness to a fixed time or to a particular subject or issue, or both.

RECORDING EVIDENCE AND THE GIVING OF REASONS

5.1 & 5.2 Omitted

5.3 The judge will make a note of the central points of the oral evidence unless it is tape recorded by the court.

5.4 The judge will make a note of the central reasons for his judgment unless it is given orally and tape recorded by the court.

5.5 (1) The judge may give his reasons as briefly and simply as the nature of the case allows.

(2) He will normally do so orally at the hearing, but he may give them later either in writing or at a hearing fixed for him to do so.

5.6 Where the judge decides the case without a hearing under rule 27.10 or a party who has given notice under rule 27.9(1) does not attend the hearing, the judge will prepare a note of his reasons and the court will send a copy to each party.

5.7 A party is entitled to a copy of any note made by the judge under sub-paragraphs 5.3 or 5.4.

5.8 Omitted

NON-ATTENDANCE OF A PARTY AT A HEARING

6.1 Attention is drawn to rule 27.9 (which enables a party to give notice that he will not attend a final hearing and sets out the effect of his giving such notice and of not doing so), and to paragraph 3 above.

6.2 Nothing in those provisions affects the general power of the court to adjourn a hearing, for example where a party who wishes to attend a hearing on the date fixed cannot do so for a good reason.

COSTS

7.1 Attention is drawn to Rule 27.14 which contains provisions about the costs which may be ordered to be paid by one party to another.

7.2 The amount which a party may be ordered to pay under rule 27.14(2)(b) (for legal advice and assistance in claims including an injunction or specific performance) is a sum not exceeding £260.

7.3 The amounts which a party may be ordered to pay under rule 27.14(3)(c) (loss of earnings) and (d) (experts' fees) are:

(1) for the loss of earnings of each party or witness due to attending a hearing or staying away from home for the purpose of attending a hearing, a sum not exceeding £50 per day for each person, and

(2) for expert's fees, a sum not exceeding £200 for each expert.

(As to recovery of pre-allocation costs in a case in which an admission by the defendant has reduced the amount in dispute to a figure below £5,000, reference should be made to paragraph 7.4 of the Practice Direction supplementing

CPR Part 26 and to paragraph 5.1(3) of the Costs Directions relating to CPR Part 44)

APPEALS

8.1 to 8.3 Omitted

Appendix A

FORM A – THE STANDARD DIRECTIONS

(for use where the district judge specifies no other directions)

THE COURT DIRECTS

1. Each party shall deliver to every other party and to the court office copies of all documents (including any experts' report) on which he intends to rely at the hearing no later than [_____] [14 days before the hearing].

2. The original documents shall be brought to the hearing.

3. [Notice of hearing date and time allowed.]

4. The court must be informed immediately if the case is settled by agreement before the hearing date.

FORM B – STANDARD DIRECTIONS FOR USE IN CLAIMS ARISING OUT OF ROAD ACCIDENTS

THE COURT DIRECTS

1. Each party shall deliver to every other party and to the court office copies of all documents on which he intends to rely at the hearing. These may include:

   • experts' reports (including medical reports where damages for personal injury are claimed),

   • witness statements,

   • invoices and estimates for repairs,

   • documents which relate to other losses, such as loss of earnings,

   • sketch plans and photographs.

2. The copies shall be delivered no later than [_____] [14 days before the hearing].

3. The original documents shall be brought to the hearing.

4. Before the date of the hearing the parties shall try to agree the cost of the repairs and any other losses claimed subject to the court's decision about whose fault the accident was.

5. Signed statements setting out the evidence of all witnesses on whom each party intends to rely shall be prepared and copies included in the documents mentioned in paragraph 1. This includes the evidence of the parties themselves and of any other witness, whether or not he is going to come to court to give evidence.

6. The parties should note that:

   (a) In deciding the case the court will find it very helpful to have a sketch plan and photographs of the place where the accident happened,

(b) The court may decide not to take into account a document or the evidence of a witness if no copy of that document or no copy of a statement or report by that witness has been supplied to the other parties.

7. [Notice of hearing date and time allowed.]

8. The court must be informed immediately if the case is settled by agreement before the hearing date.

FORM C – STANDARD DIRECTIONS FOR USE IN CLAIMS ARISING OUT OF BUILDING DISPUTES, VEHICLE REPAIRS AND SIMILAR CONTRACTUAL CLAIMS

THE COURT DIRECTS

1. Each party shall deliver to every other party and to the court office copies of all documents on which he intends to rely at the hearing. These may include:

   - the contract,

   - witness statements,

   - experts' reports,

   - photographs,

   - invoices for work done or goods supplied,

   - estimates for work to be done.

2. The copies shall be delivered no later than [_____] [14 days before the hearing].

3. The original documents shall be brought to the hearing.

4. [The_____shall deliver to the_____and to the court office [no later than_____] [with his copy documents] a list showing all items of work which he complains about and why, and the amount claimed for putting each item right.]

5. [The _____ shall deliver to the_____and to the court office [no later than _____] [with his copy documents] a breakdown of the amount he is claiming showing all work done and materials supplied.]

6. Before the date of the hearing the parties shall try to agree about the nature and cost of any

remedial work required, subject to the court's decision about any other issue in the case.

7. [Signed statements setting out the evidence of all witnesses on whom each party intends to rely shall be prepared and included in the documents mentioned in paragraph 1. This includes the evidence of the parties themselves and of any other witness, whether or not he is going to come to court to give evidence.]

8. The parties should note that:

    (a) in deciding the case the judge may find it helpful to have photographs showing the work in question,

    (b) the judge may decide not to take into account a document or the evidence of a witness if no copy of that document or no copy of a statement or report by that witness has been supplied to the other parties.

9. [Notice of hearing date and time allowed.]

10. The court must be informed immediately if the case is settled by agreement before the hearing date.

11. FORM D – TENANTS' CLAIMS FOR THE RETURN OF DEPOSITS/LANDLORDS CLAIMS FOR DAMAGE CAUSED

THE COURT DIRECTS

1. Each party shall deliver to every other party and to the court office copies of all documents on which he intends to rely at the hearing. These may include:

   - the tenancy agreement and any inventory,

   - the rent book or other evidence of rent and other payments made by the to _____ the _____,

   - photographs,

   - witness statements,

   - invoices or estimates for work and goods.

2. The copies shall be delivered no later than [_____] [14 days before the hearing].

3. The original documents shall be brought to the hearing.

4. The _____ shall deliver with his copy documents a list showing each item of loss or damage for which he claims the _____ ought to pay, and the amount he claims for the replacement or repair.

5. The parties shall before the hearing date try to agree about the nature and cost of any repairs and replacements needed, subject to the court's decision about any other issue in the case.

6. [Signed statements setting out the evidence of all witnesses on whom each party intends to rely shall be prepared and included in the documents mentioned in paragraph 1. This includes the evidence of the parties themselves

and of any other witness whether or not he is going to come to court to give evidence.]

7. The parties should note that: a) in deciding the case the judge may find it helpful to have photographs showing the condition of the property, b) the judge may decide not to take into account a document or the evidence of a witness if no copy of that document or no copy of a statement or report by that witness has been supplied to the other parties.

8. [Notice of hearing date and time allowed.]

9. The court must be informed immediately if the case is settled by agreement before the hearing date.

FORM E – HOLIDAY AND WEDDING CLAIMS

THE COURT DIRECTS

1. Each party shall deliver to every other party and to the court office copies of all documents on which he intends to rely at the hearing. These may include:

   - any written contract, brochure or booking form,

   - photographs,

   - documents showing payments made,

   - witness statements,

   - letters.

2. The copies shall be delivered no later than [_____] [14 days before the hearing].

3. The original documents shall be brought to the hearing.

4. Signed statements setting out the evidence of all witnesses on whom each party intends to rely shall be prepared and copies included in the documents mentioned in paragraph 1. This includes the evidence of the parties themselves and of any other witness, whether or not he is going to come to court to give evidence.

5. If either party intends to show a video as evidence he must:

   (a) contact the court at once to make arrangements for him to do so, because the court may not have the necessary equipment, and

   (b) provide the other party with a copy of the video or the opportunity to see it (if he asks) at least 2 weeks before the hearing.

130

6. The parties should note that the court may decide not to take into account a document or the evidence of a witness or a video if these directions have not been complied with.

7. [Notice of hearing date and time allowed.]

8. The court must be told immediately if the case is settled by agreement before the hearing date.

FORM F – SOME SPECIAL DIRECTIONS

The _____ must clarify his case. He must do this by delivering to the court office and to the no later than

[a list of _____]

[details of_____]

[_____]

The_____shall allow the _____ to inspect _____ by appointment within _____ days of receiving a request to do so.

The hearing will not take place at the court but at _____.

The _____ must bring to court at the hearing the _____.

Signed statements setting out the evidence of all witnesses on whom each party intends to rely shall be prepared and copies included in the documents mentioned in paragraph 1. This includes the evidence of the parties themselves and of any other witness, whether or not he is going to come to court to give evidence.

The court may decide not to take into account a document [or video] or the evidence of a witness if these directions have not been complied with.

If he does not [do so] _____] his [Claim] [Defence] [and Counterclaim] and will be struck out and [(specify consequence)]. It appears to the court that expert evidence is necessary on the issue of

_____]

and that that evidence should be given by a single expert

_____]

to be instructed by the parties jointly. If the parties cannot agree about who to chose and what arrangements to make about paying his fee, either party may apply to the court for further directions. If either party intends to show a video as evidence he must

(a)   contact the court at once to make arrangements for him to do so, because the court may not have the necessary equipment, and

(b)   provide the other party with a copy of the video or the opportunity to see it at least_____] before the hearing.

APPENDIX 2

EXAMPLE PLEADINGS

Example 1

PARTICULARS OF CLAIM

---

1.   The Defendants are and were at all material times in the business c selling cleaning products.

2.   On the 7th February 1996 the Defendants in the course of the sai business contracted with the Claimant and sold 4 bottles of "miracle clean detergent at a price of £99.

3.   At the time of the said contract the Claimant told the Defendants tha the said detergent would be used for the purpose of cleaning the curtains an carpets at his flat at 10, Gillespie Drive, Warwickshire.

4.   It was an implied term of the said contract that the said deterger should be :

   a)   reasonably fit for the said purpose

   b)   of satisfactory quality.

5.   On the 10th February the Claimant used the said detergent to clea curtains and carpets at his flat.

6.   In breach of the said implied terms the said detergent was not fit for th required purpose and was not of satisfactory quality in that it damaged th

Claimant's curtains and carpets beyond repair. The said curtains and carpets lost their colour and developed large holes.

7.   By reason of the matters aforesaid the Claimant has suffered loss and damage.

PARTICULARS OF DAMAGE

1)	Value of carpets	£1,000
2)	Cost of removing the old carpets and fitting new carpets	£ 200
3)	Value of curtains	£ 300

£1,500

AND the Claimant claims

1)   Damages

2)   Interest

3)   Costs

———————————————

DEFENCE AND COUNTERCLAIM

———————————————

1.   Paragraphs 1, 2, 3 and 4 of the Particulars of Claim are admitted.

2.   Paragraph 5 is not admitted.

3.   It is denied that the Defendants were in breach of the said implied

terms as alleged in paragraph 6 of the Particulars of Claim or at all. In particular it is denied that the damage was caused by the said detergent. Alternatively if the damage was caused by the said detergent it is averred that this was a result of the Claimant's failure to follow the instructions for use printed on the bottles.

4.   No admission is made as to the alleged or any loss and damage or the amount thereof. It is denied that any loss and damage suffered by the Claimant was caused by any breach of contract by the Defendants.

5.   If contrary to their Defence the Defendants are held liable to the Claimant they will seek to set off so much of the sum counterclaimed herein as may extinguish or diminish such liability.

COUNTERCLAIM

6.   Paragraph 1 hereof is repeated.

7.   On the 14th February 1996 the Defendants by their invoice No. 6966 demanded from the Claimant the sum of £99 pursuant to the said contract. Despite frequent requests, oral and written, for payment the Claimant has not paid the Defendant the said sum or any part thereof.

AND the Defendants claim

1)   £99

2)   Interest

Example 2

PARTICULARS OF CLAIM

---

1.   On 13th April 1995 at about 10 pm the Claimant was walking across Parsons Road when the Defendant drove his Range Rover car registration number .... from Widney Avenue onto Parsons Road, hit the Claimant and knocked him down.

2.   The accident was caused by the negligence of the Defendant.

PARTICULARS OF NEGLIGENCE

The Defendant was negligent in that he

a)   drove too fast in all the circumstances

b)   failed to keep any, or any proper look-out

c)   failed to stop, slow down, steer or otherwise control his car so as to avoid hitting the Claimant

3.   As a result of the said accident the Claimant suffered pain, injury, loss and damage.

PARTICULARS OF INJURY

a)   sprained left wrist

b)   bruises

c)   pain and shock

Further particulars of the Claimant's injuries are set out in the medical report served herewith.

PARTICULARS OF SPECIAL DAMAGE

a)   Broken wrist watch   £ 60

b)   Loss of earnings   £100

AND the Claimant claims

1)   Damages

2)   Interest

3)   Costs

DEFENCE

---

1.   Paragraph 1 is admitted.

2.   The Defendant denies that he was negligent as alleged or at all or that the said accident was caused by any negligence on his part.

3.   The said accident was caused solely by or contributed to by the negligence of the Claimant

PARTICULARS OF NEGLIGENCE

a)   Failing to look or look properly before stepping out

b)   Failing to observe the Defendant's car

c)   Failing to stop, step aside or take any other action to avoid being struck by the Defendant's car

4.   No admission is made as to the alleged or any pain, injury, loss or damage or as to the amount thereof.

APPENDIX 3

Forms Cited in Text

N1	Claim Form
N1A	Notes for claimant
N1C	Notes for defendant
N1(FD)	Consumer Credit Act Claim
N9	Response Pack
N9A	Form of admission and statement of means to accompany Form N1
N9B	Defence and Counterclaim (specified amount)
N9C	Admission (unspecified amount, non-money and return of goods claim)
N10	Notice that Acknowledgement of Service has been filed
N150	Allocation Questionnaire
N152	Notice that a [Defence] [Counterclaim] has been filed
N153	Notice of Allocation or Listing Hearing
N157	Notice of Allocation to the Small Claims Track
N158	Notice of Allocation to the Small Claims Track (preliminary hearing)
N159	Notice of Allocation to the Small Claims Track (no hearing)
N205A	Notice of Issue (specified amount) and request for judgement
N205B	Notice of Issue (unspecified amount) and request for judgement
N211	Claim Form (Part 20)
N211A	Notes for claimant
N211C	Notes for defendant
N212	Notice of Issue
N213	Acknowledgement of Service

N215	Certificate of Service
N225	Request for Judgement and reply to Admission (specified amount)
N225A	Notice of Part Admission (specified amount)
N226	Notice of Admission (unspecified amount)
N227	Request for Judgement by Default 9amount to be decided by the court)
N236	Notice of Defence that Amount claimed has been paid – Claimant's reply
N244	Application Notice
N279	Notice of Discontinuance

OTHER FORMS TO CONSIDER

Consumer Credit Act Claim: Time Order AND Extortionate Credit Bargain

Assured Shorthold Tenancy

Charging Order form